flashcards and quick questions

AQA PSYCHOLOGY
FOR A LEVEL YEAR 1 & AS

Flashbook

Cara Flanagan
Rob Liddle
Arwa Mohamedbhai

Published in 2017 by Illuminate Publishing Ltd,
P.O. Box 1160, Cheltenham, Gloucestershire GL50 9RW

Orders: Please visit www.illuminatepublishing.com
or email sales@illuminatepublishing.com

British Library Cataloguing in Publication Data

A catalogue record for this book is available from the British Library

ISBN 978-1-911208-40-2

Printed in the UK by Cambrian Printers, Aberystwyth

11.17

The publisher's policy is to use papers that are natural, renewable
and recyclable products made from wood grown in sustainable
forests. The logging and manufacturing processes are expected to
conform to the environmental regulations of the country of origin.

Editor: Geoff Tuttle

Design and layout: Nigel Harriss

AO1

AO3

Book-link

Y1/AS Student Book
Pages 16–17

Y1/AS Revision Guide
Pages 10–11

Spec Spotlight
Types of
conformity:
internalisation,
identification and
compliance.
Explanations for
conformity: informational
social influence and
normative social
influence.

Types of conformity

Internalisation is accepting group norms.

Identification is wanting to be like the group,
public change.

Compliance is public change only.

Explanations for conformity

Informational social influence (ISI) is about
information, desire to be right.

Normative social influence (NSI) is about
norms, desire to be like others and not look
foolish.

⊕ Support for ISI – hard maths problems,
more conformity (Lucas *et al.*).

⊖ ISI individual differences – students less
conformist (28% vs 37%, Asch).

⊖ Two-process approach oversimplified –
not necessarily ISI or NSI.

⊕ Support for NSI – conformity fell to 12.5%
when answers written (Asch).

⊖ NSI individual differences – nAffiliators
more conformist (McGhee and Teevan).

Conformity: types and explanations – multiple choice questions

1 Genuinely accepting group norms is called:
(a) Compliance.
(b) Identification.
(c) Internalisation.

2 Compliance is a:
(a) Public change of view only.
(b) Public and private change of behaviour.
(c) Permanent change.

3 ISI is:
(a) Internalised social influence.
(b) Individual social influence.
(c) Informational social influence.

4 NSI is most likely when you:
(a) Know what the group norms are.
(b) Want to be liked.
(c) Want to be right.

5 Lucas *et al.*'s study:
(a) Shows need for social approval.
(b) Supports the role of ISI.
(c) Shows individual differences in conformity.

6 Two-process approach assumes:
(a) ISI is more important than NSI.
(b) NSI is more common than ISI.
(c) ISI and NSI are independent.

7 The finding that conformity drops when answers are written:
(a) Supports NSI.
(b) Supports ISI.
(c) Supports NSI and ISI.

8 nAffiliators are:
(a) More affected by ISI.
(b) More affected by NSI.
(c) Equally affected by NSI and ISI.

Answers
1C 2A 3C 4B
5B 6C 7A 8B

Possible extended writing questions:

- Discuss normative social influence as an explanation for conformity. *[AS = 12, AL = 16]*
- Outline and evaluate informational social influence **and** normative social influence as explanations for conformity. *[AS = 12, AL = 16]*

Book-link

Y1/AS Student Book
Pages 18–19

Y1/AS Revision Guide
Pages 12–13

Spec Spotlight

Variables affecting
conformity including
group size, unanimity
and task difficulty as
investigated by Asch.

Asch baseline study

Procedure – line length task, 123 American students, confederates gave wrong answers.

Findings – naïve participants conformed 36.8% of the time, 75% at least once.

Conclusion – most participants conformed to avoid rejection (NSI).

Variables affecting conformity

Group size – three confederates 31.8% conformity, more made little difference.

Unanimity – presence of dissenter reduced conformity.

Task difficulty – conformity increased with harder task, showing ISI.

⊖ Asch study 'child of its time' – later study no conformity (Perrin and Spencer).

⊖ Artificial situation and task – trivial and not a 'real' group so not generalisable.

⊖ Limited application of findings – more conformity in collectivist cultures (Bond and Smith).

⊖ Only applies to some situations – more conformity in groups of friends (Williams and Sogon).

⊖ Ethical issues – e.g. participants deceived (but weigh up against benefits).

1 The task in Asch's study involved:
(a) Electric shocks.
(b) Lines.
(c) Maths problems.

2 Asch's participants were:
(a) American students.
(b) Males and females.
(c) People in a wide variety of jobs.

3 How many comparison lines per card were there?
(a) 2
(b) 3
(c) 4

4 The conformity rate in the baseline study was:
(a) 31.8%
(b) 36.8%
(c) 75%

5 Asch did *not* investigate:
(a) Group size.
(b) Degree of unanimity.
(c) Gender of participants.

6 Bond and Smith argued conformity is:
(a) Lower in males than in females.
(b) Higher in collectivist cultures than in individualist ones.
(c) Higher in groups of strangers than in groups of friends.

7 Williams and Sogon found more conformity:
(a) Between strangers.
(b) In 1980s students.
(c) In groups of friends.

8 Asch's study was unethical because:
(a) There was no debriefing.
(b) Participants were deceived.
(c) Some participants were physically harmed.

Topic 1: SOCIAL INFLUENCE

Answers
1B 2A 3B 4B
5C 6B 7C 8B

Possible extended writing questions:

- Describe and evaluate **two or more** variables affecting conformity, as investigated by Asch. *[AS = 12, AL = 16]*.
- Discuss Asch's research into conformity. *[AS = 12, AL = 16]*

Conformity to social roles: Zimbardo's research

A01 **A03**

Y1/AS Student Book
Pages 20–21

Y1/AS Revision Guide
Pages 14–15

Spec Spotlight

Conformity to social roles as investigated by Zimbardo.

Procedure

Stanford Prison Experiment (SPE), student volunteers in mock prison.

Randomly allocated to roles, guards had complete power.

Prisoners and guards de-individuated (e.g. uniforms) to lose personal identity.

Findings and conclusions

Guards identified with role and became increasingly more aggressive.

Prisoners rebelled but passive after guards responded, SPE ended early (after 5 days).

Everyone conformed to their social roles, i.e. power of situation.

⊕ Control of variables (e.g. allocation of roles) – increased internal validity.

⊖ Lack of realism – participants play-acted stereotypes (Banuazizi and Mohaved).

⊖ Understated dispositional influences – e.g. personality (Fromm).

⊖ Contradicted by subsequent research – BBC study supported social identity theory (Reicher and Haslam).

⊖ Ethical issues – conflict between Zimbardo's two roles (prison superintendent and lead researcher).

1 Zimbardo's participants were:
(a) Female.
(b) Emotionally unstable.
(c) Volunteers.

2 The method used to allocate roles was:
(a) Systematic.
(b) Opportunity sampling.
(c) Random.

3 De-individuation means:
(a) Identifying with your role.
(b) Losing your sense of personal identity.
(c) Becoming more aggressive.

4 The prisoners in the SPE:
(a) Were depressed throughout.
(b) Did not conform to their role.
(c) Initially rebelled but then became passive.

5 The findings demonstrate:
(a) The influence of personality.
(b) The power of situational factors.
(c) That social roles are irrelevant.

6 Control of variables in the SPE:
(a) Showed the importance of dispositional factors.
(b) Increased internal validity.
(c) Increased internal and external validity.

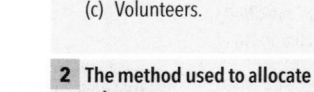

7 The BBC prison study:
(a) Supported social identity theory.
(b) Supported Milgram's conclusions.
(c) Did not address conformity to social roles.

8 In the SPE, Zimbardo was:
(a) Prison superintendent and lead researcher.
(b) Lead researcher only.
(c) One of the guards.

Topic 1: SOCIAL INFLUENCE

Answers
1C 2C 3B 4C
5B 6B 7A 8A

Possible extended writing questions:

- Discuss conformity to social roles, as investigated by Zimbardo. *[AS = 12, AL = 16]*
- Describe and evaluate Zimbardo's research into conformity to social roles. *[AS = 12, AL = 16]*

Obedience: Milgram's research

Book-link

Y1/AS Student Book
Pages 22–23

Y1/AS Revision Guide
Pages 16–17

Spec Spotlight

Obedience as
investigated
by Milgram.

AO1

Procedure

Naïve male volunteers gave 'shocks' to a
'learner' (Mr Wallace).

An experimenter ordered participants to
continue giving shocks.

Shock machine started at 15 volts and went up
in 15 V steps to 450 V.

Findings and conclusions

All participants gave at least 300 V, 65% gave
450 V, showed stress.

Prior to the study, survey of 14 students
predicted 3% would give 450 V.

Participants debriefed, 84% reported that they
felt glad to have participated.

AO3

⊖ Lacks internal validity – participants
guessed shocks fake (Orne and Holland).

⊕ High external validity – processes in lab
same as outside (e.g. Hofling *et al.*).

⊕ Support from replications – e.g. French
reality TV show, 80% went to 450 V.

⊖ SIT is alternative theory – participants
gave shocks because identified with the
experimenter (Haslam and Reicher).

⊖ Ethical issues – e.g. deception betrays
trust in research (Baumrind).

Obedience: Milgram's research – multiple choice questions

1 Milgram's participants were:
(a) Males.
(b) Various nationalities.
(c) Students.

2 'Mr Wallace' was:
(a) The 'Teacher'.
(b) The 'Experimenter'.
(c) The 'Learner'.

3 The 'shocks' increased each time by:
(a) 15 volts.
(b) 30 volts.
(c) 45 volts.

4 The proportion of completely obedient participants was:
(a) 15%
(b) 65%
(c) 100%

5 84% of the participants:
(a) Said they were glad they had taken part.
(b) Were debriefed.
(c) Refused to obey.

6 Replication in a French reality TV programme found maximum shock given by:
(a) 60%
(b) 70%
(c) 80%

7 The external validity of Milgram's study is supported by:
(a) Orne and Holland.
(b) Baumrind.
(c) Hofling *et al.*

8 Haslam and Reicher explain Milgram's findings in terms of:
(a) Ethical issues.
(b) Social identity theory.
(c) Participants realising the shocks were fake.

Topic 1: SOCIAL INFLUENCE

Answers
1A 2C 3A 4B
5A 6C 7C 8B

Possible extended writing questions:
• Discuss research into obedience. *[AS = 12, AL = 16]*
• Describe and evaluate Milgram's research into obedience. *[AS = 12, AL = 16]*

Book-link

Y1/AS Student Book
Pages 24–25

Y1/AS Revision Guide
Pages 18–19

Spec Spotlight

Explanations
for obedience:
situational variables
affecting obedience
including proximity,
location and uniform,
as investigated
by Milgram.

Proximity

Teacher and learner in same room, obedience fell from 65% to 40%.

Touch proximity – teacher forced learner's hand on plate, 30% obedience.

Remote instruction proximity – orders from experimenter over phone, 20.5% obedience.

Location

Experiment conducted in run-down building, 47.5% obedience.

Uniform

Member of public in everyday clothes gave orders, 20% obedience.

⊕ Research support – uniform conveys authority/increases obedience (Bickman).

⊖ Low internal validity – participants knew procedure fake (Orne and Holland).

⊕ Supported by replications – e.g. in other cultures (although mostly Western).

⊕ High control of variables – Milgram altered one variable at a time.

⊖ 'Obedience alibi' – blaming situational factors ignores racism, etc. (Mandel).

1 Obedience with teacher and learner in same room was:
(a) 40%
(b) 47.5%
(c) 65%

2 Obedience when experimenter gave orders over phone was:
(a) 10%
(b) 20.5%
(c) 30%

3 Obedience with study done in a run-down building was:
(a) 30%
(b) 40%
(c) 47.5%

4 Obedience when a 'member of the public' gave orders was:
(a) 10%
(b) 20%
(c) 30%

5 Bickman investigated the role of:
(a) Proximity.
(b) Social support.
(c) Uniforms.

6 Milgram's variations may lack internal validity because:
(a) They have ethical issues.
(b) There are no replications.
(c) Participants realised the shocks were fake.

7 External validity is high because:
(a) SIT can explain the results.
(b) Findings have been replicated in other cultures.
(c) Findings are not generalisable.

8 Mandel criticised situational explanations for:
(a) Providing an 'obedience alibi'.
(b) Lacking external validity.
(c) Ignoring social influences.

Answers
1A 2B 3C 4B
5C 6C 7B 8A

Possible extended writing questions:

- Describe and evaluate **two** explanations for obedience. *[AS = 12, AL = 16]*
- Discuss **one or more** situational variables affecting obedience. *[AS = 12, AL = 16]*

Spec Spotlight

Explanations for
obedience: agentic
state and legitimacy
of authority.

Agentic state

Become 'agent' of authority, losing personal
responsibility.

Switch from autonomous to agentic state is
called agentic shift.

Binding factors reduce moral strain and
ignore damaging effects of obedience.

⊕ Research support – students saw
participants as agents of experimenter
(Blass and Schmidt).

⊖ Limited explanation – e.g. nurses in Hofling
et al. didn't show anxiety.

⊖ Limited explanation – can't explain
disobedience in Battalion 101 (Mandel).

Legitimacy of authority

Accept some people's authority, agreed by
society.

Hand over control to trusted authority,
learned to do so in childhood.

History shows leaders often use legitimate
authority destructively.

⊕ Cultural differences in obedience – reflect
differences in legitimacy, e.g. Germans 85%
obedient (Mantell).

⊕ Explains real-life obedience – e.g. US Army
hierarchy in My Lai massacre.

Topic 1: SOCIAL INFLUENCE

Obedience: Social-psychological factors – multiple choice questions

1 When in an agentic state, you:
(a) Take personal responsibility.
(b) Act according to your conscience.
(c) May obey destructive authority.

2 The opposite of agentic state is:
(a) Dependent state.
(b) Obedient state.
(c) Autonomous state.

3 Aspects of a situation that reduce 'moral strain' are called:
(a) Agentic factors.
(b) Autonomous factors.
(c) Binding factors.

4 Legitimate authority is:
(a) The same in all cultures.
(b) Socially accepted and approved.
(c) Always used constructively.

5 Hofling et al. (1966) investigated obedience in:
(a) Nurses.
(b) Doctors.
(c) Nazi soldiers.

6 A small number of the Nazi reserve police in Battalion 101 showed:
(a) Obedience to authority.
(b) Disobedience.
(c) An agentic shift.

7 Legitimacy of authority is a good explanation of:
(a) Cultural differences in obedience.
(b) Real-life obedience.
(c) Both of the above.

8 A good example of real-life obedience is:
(a) Milgram's procedures.
(b) Asch's findings.
(c) The massacre at My Lai.

Answers
1C 2C 3C 4B
5A 6B 7C 8C

Possible extended writing questions:

- Discuss **one or more** explanations for obedience. *[AS = 12, AL = 16]*
- Describe and evaluate agentic state **or** legitimacy of authority as an explanation for obedience. *[AS = 12, AL = 16]*

Obedience: Dispositional explanations

Y1/AS Student Book
Pages 28–29
Y1/AS Revision Guide
Pages 22–23

Spec Spotlight

Dispositional explanations for obedience: the authoritarian personality.

Authoritarian personality

Adorno *et al.* – unquestionning obedience is pathological.

Extreme respect to authority, contempt for 'inferiors', conventional attitudes.

Originates in childhood through strict parenting and conditional love.

Child's hostility to parents displaced onto weaker others, called scapegoating.

Key study: Adorno *et al.*

Procedure – F-Scale measured authoritarianism of 2000 Americans.

Findings – high scorers showed deference to people of higher status.

⊕ Research support – links obedience and authoritarianism (Elms and Milgram).

⊖ Limited explanation – many Germans anti-Semitic but not same personality.

⊖ Political bias – F-scale can't explain left-wing authoritarianism (Christie and Jahoda).

⊖ Methodology – F-scale flawed so theory lacks validity (Greenstein).

⊖ Correlational research – measures many variables but no cause and effect.

Topic 1: SOCIAL INFLUENCE

Obedience: Dispositional explanations – *multiple choice questions*

1 A key feature of authoritarian personality is:
(a) Extreme respect for authority.
(b) Respect for social 'inferiors'.
(c) Hatred of social hierarchies.

2 Authoritarian personality is caused by:
(a) Social roles.
(b) Unconditional love.
(c) Harsh parenting in childhood.

3 Displacing hostility onto weaker others is called:
(a) Scapelambing.
(b) Scapepuppying.
(c) Scapegoating.

4 Adorno *et al.* studied 2000:
(a) Americans.
(b) Working-class people.
(c) Females.

5 Links between authoritarian personality and obedience are:
(a) Mostly correlational.
(b) Usually cause-and-effect.
(c) Non-existent.

6 Authoritarian personality solely explains:
(a) Nazism in Germany.
(b) Right-wing authoritarianism.
(c) All obedience.

7 The F-scale is politically biased because it:
(a) Only explains anti-Semitism.
(b) Does not measure left-wing authoritarianism.
(c) Is a questionnaire.

8 The theory lacks validity because:
(a) The F-scale is flawed.
(b) Research is experimental.
(c) It is a situational explanation.

Topic 1: SOCIAL INFLUENCE

Answers
1A 2C 3C 4A
5A 6B 7B 8A

Possible extended writing questions:

- Outline and evaluate the authoritarian personality as an explanation for obedience. *[AS = 12, AL = 16]*
- Describe and evaluate **one** dispositional explanation for obedience. Refer to **one other** explanation in your answer. *[AS = 12, AL = 16]*

Topic 1: SOCIAL INFLUENCE

Social support

| Conformity reduces if a peer dissents (Asch) because they act as a model. | ⊕ | Research support – conformity reduced when one dissented (Allen and Levine). |

| Effect is temporary – naïve participant conforms again if dissenter conforms. | ⊕ | Research support – participants less obedient with support (Gamson *et al.*). |

| Obedience reduces if one dissenter (Milgram study 65% down to 10%). | | |

Spec Spotlight

Explanations of resistance to social influence including social support and locus of control.

Locus of control (LoC)

| Internals place control within themselves, externals place it outside. | ⊕ | Research support – more externals continued to highest shock (Holland). |

| There is a continuum from high internal → low internal → low external → high external. | ⊖ | Contradictory research – people now more independent but also more external (Twenge *et al.*). |

| Internals can resist social influence, more confident, less need for approval. | ⊖ | LoC exaggerated – only influential in new situations, so limited (Rotter). |

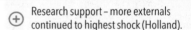

1 Peer support leads to reduced conformity because:
(a) The peer is correct.
(b) Peers are always less conformist.
(c) The peer acts as a model.

2 In Milgram, when one person disobeyed, obedience reduced to:
(a) 10%
(b) 20%
(c) 30%

3 Internals believe things that happen are due mainly to:
(a) Their own hard work.
(b) Their intelligence.
(c) Circumstances.

4 Most likely to resist social influence are:
(a) Low externals.
(b) High internals.
(c) Low internals.

5 Gamson *et al.* found that social support:
(a) Reduced obedience.
(b) Reduced conformity.
(c) Had no effect.

6 Holland found the highest shocks were given by:
(a) Externals.
(b) Internals.
(c) Independents.

7 As people have become more external they have also surprisingly become:
(a) More obedient.
(b) Less conformist.
(c) More independent.

8 Locus of control affects resistance to social influence in:
(a) Stressful situations.
(b) New situations.
(c) All situations.

Answers
1C 2A 3A 4B
5A 6A 7C 8B

Possible extended writing questions:

- Outline and evaluate **one or more** explanations of resistance to social influence. *[AS = 12, AL = 16]*
- Discuss social support as an explanation of resistance to social influence. *[AS = 12, AL = 16]*
- Discuss locus of control as an explanation of resistance to social influence. *[AS = 12, AL = 16]*

Y1/AS Student Book
Pages 32–33
Y1/AS Revision Guide
Pages 26–27

Internalisation – with minority influence private as well as public view is changed.

Consistency – synchronic and diachronic, makes others rethink their own views.

Commitment – helps gain attention. e.g. through extreme activities (augmentation).

Flexibility – avoid rigidity, accept reasonable counter-arguments.

Snowball effect – minority over time becomes majority through conversion.

Spec Spotlight

Minority influence including reference to consistency, commitment and flexibility.

Key study: Moscovici et al.

Procedure – 36 blue-green slides identified as green consistently or inconsistently.

Findings – consistent minority led to same wrong answer on 8.42% of trials, inconsistent minority led to 1.25%.

$\oplus$ Research support – consistent minorities are influential (Wood et al., meta-analysis).

$\oplus$ Research support – minority's messages processed more deeply (Martin et al.).

$\ominus$ Artificial tasks – unlike real life so studies lack external validity.

$\oplus$ Support for internalisation – minority more influential when answers written.

$\ominus$ Limited application – in real life minority/majority situations more complicated, e.g. majorities have status not just more numbers.

Topic 1: SOCIAL INFLUENCE

1 **Minority influence occurs mainly through:**
   (a) Compliance.
   (b) Internalisation.
   (c) Obedience.

2 **Influential minorities must be:**
   (a) Sometimes flexible.
   (b) Almost as big as the majority.
   (c) Consistent and committed all the time.

3 **A minority becomes the majority over time through the:**
   (a) Snowball effect.
   (b) Consistency effect.
   (c) Conversion effect.

4 **Moscovici et al. found participants agreed with a consistent majority:**
   (a) 1.25% of the time.
   (b) 8.42% of the time.
   (c) 32% of the time.

5 **The methodology used by Wood et al. was a:**
   (a) Laboratory experiment.
   (b) Questionnaire.
   (c) Meta-analysis.

6 **Martin et al. found that messages from minorities are:**
   (a) Nearly always ineffective.
   (b) Usually readily accepted.
   (c) Processed deeply.

7 **Studies using artificial tasks:**
   (a) Lack external validity.
   (b) Have high internal validity.
   (c) Tell us a lot about real-life minority influence.

8 **The task in Moscovici et al.'s study involved identifying the colour of:**
   (a) 50 blue slides.
   (b) 36 blue-green slides.
   (c) 36 blue slides.

Answers
1B 2A 3A 4B
5C 6C 7A 8B

Possible extended writing questions:

- Discuss research into minority influence. Refer to 'commitment' **and** 'flexibility' in your answer. *[AS = 12, AL = 16]*
- Discuss research into consistency, commitment **and** flexibility in relation to minority influence. *[AS = 12, AL = 16]*

Book-link

Y1/AS Student Book
Pages 34–35

Y1/AS Revision Guide
Pages 28–29

Spec Spotlight

The role of social
influence processes in
social change.

Lessons from minority influence

Civil rights minority marching with consistent message draws attention to social issue.

⊖ Minority influence indirect – also delayed, so narrow role (Nemeth).

Consistent minority forces majority to think more deeply about issue.

⊖ Deeper processing – majorities think as deeply as minorities so challenges Moscovici (Mackie).

Minority becomes majority (snowball effect), source of change forgotten (social cryptomnesia).

⊖ Identification – identifying with minority overlooked in research (Bashir et al.).

Lessons from conformity

Dissenter breaks power of majority, and also appeal to NSI.

⊕ Support for NSI – reduced people's energy use (Nolan et al.).

Lessons from obedience

Disobedient model promotes social change, gradual commitment helps.

⊖ Methodological issues – theories based on flawed studies (Milgram, Asch, etc.).

1 When minorities march and demonstrate, they:
(a) Cause a snowball effect.
(b) Create social change.
(c) Draw attention to an issue.

2 A minority is influential when it:
(a) Presents a view consistently.
(b) Ignores counter-arguments.
(c) Applies pressure to conform.

3 Social cryptomnesia occurs when:
(a) A minority has no influence.
(b) The majority forgets the source of a social change.
(c) A minority becomes the majority.

4 Disobedient people promote social change because they:
(a) Are always right.
(b) Provide a model.
(c) Have strong personalities.

5 Nolan et al. promoted social change by using:
(a) NSI.
(b) ISI.
(c) Compliance.

6 Nemeth argues the effects of minority influence are:
(a) Immediate.
(b) Linked to the central issue.
(c) Delayed and indirect.

7 Bashir et al. argue that minority influence requires:
(a) Obedience.
(b) Conformity.
(c) Identification with the minority.

8 Theories of social influence:
(a) Are based on flawed studies.
(b) Are extremely valid.
(c) Explain most examples of social change.

Topic 1: SOCIAL INFLUENCE

Answers
1C 2A 3B 4B
5A 6C 7C 8A

Possible extended writing questions:

• Outline and evaluate the role of social influence processes in social change. *[AS = 12, AL = 16]*
• Discuss the role of **two** social influence processes in social change. *[AS = 12, AL = 16]*

Coding, capacity, duration of memory

Book-link

Y1/AS Student Book
Pages 46–47

Y1/AS Revision Guide
Pages 30–31

Spec Spotlight

Short-term memory
and long-term memory.
Features of each store:
coding, capacity and
duration.

Coding

Baddeley – STM coding acoustic (sounds), LTM coding semantic (meaning).

⊖ Baddeley's materials not very realistic – so study has limited generalisability.

Capacity

Jacobs – STM capacity 9.3 numbers and 7.3 letters on average.

⊖ Jacob's study conducted long ago – lacked control of extraneous variables.

Miller – STM capacity is 7 ± 2 items on average (increased by chunking).

⊖ Miller overestimated STM capacity – 4 chunks may be the average (Cowan).

Duration

Peterson and Peterson – STM duration 18–30 seconds without rehearsal.

⊖ Artificial materials (consonant syllables) mean low external validity.

Bahrick *et al.* – LTM duration 70% accurate photo recognition after 48 years.

⊕ Bahrick's study high external validity – tested real-life meaningful memories.

Topic 2: MEMORY

1 Coding in STM is mostly:
(a) Visual.
(b) Semantic.
(c) Acoustic.

2 Capacity of STM was studied by:
(a) Peterson and Peterson.
(b) Miller.
(c) Baddeley.

3 Duration of STM is about:
(a) Several minutes.
(b) Half a minute.
(c) Several hours.

4 Bahrick et al. found accuracy of photo recognition was:
(a) 70% after 48 years.
(b) 35% after 48 years.
(c) 25% after 30 years.

5 Baddeley used:
(a) Not very realistic materials.
(b) Real-life memory tasks.
(c) Nonsense syllables.

6 Lack of control in Jacob's study may have led to:
(a) High validity.
(b) Good generalisability.
(c) Extraneous variables.

7 Cowan argues STM capacity is:
(a) 7 ± 2 items on average.
(b) 4 chunks on average.
(c) Practically unlimited.

8 Peterson and Peterson used lists of:
(a) Consonant syllables.
(b) Shopping items.
(c) Phone numbers.

Answers
1C 2B 3B 4A
5A 6C 7B 8A

Possible extended writing questions:
• Outline and evaluate research into **three** features of short-term memory. *[AS =12, AL = 16]*
• Discuss research into short-term memory. In your answer refer to capacity **and** duration. *[AS =12, AL = 16]*

Y1/AS Student Book
Pages 48–49

Y1/AS Revision Guide
Pages 32–33

MSM Describes three separate memory stores, linked by processing.

Sensory register (SR) – brief duration, high capacity, coding varies with sense.

Transfer SR to STM – only small amount of information attended to is passed on.

Short-term memory (STM) – capacity is 5 to 9 items, duration is 18–30 seconds, coding is acoustic.

Transfer STM to LTM – occurs through maintenance rehearsal.

Long-term memory (LTM) – capacity is unlimited, duration is up to lifetime, coding is semantic.

Retrieval via STM.

⊕ Research support – STM and LTM are different (e.g. coding, Baddeley).

⊖ Can't explain more than one type of STM in amnesic KF (Shallice and Warrington).

⊖ More than one type of rehearsal – e.g. elaborative (Craik and Watkins).

⊖ Supporting studies use artificial materials – e.g. consonant syllables.

⊖ MSM oversimplifies LTM – research shows different types of LTM.

Spec Spotlight

The multi-store model of memory: sensory register, short-term memory and long-term memory. Features of each store: coding, capacity and duration.

25

Multi-store model of memory (MSM) – multiple choice questions

1 The sensory register:
(a) Has very brief duration.
(b) Is low capacity.
(c) Always uses acoustic coding.

2 Transfer from SR to STM requires:
(a) Attention.
(b) Rehearsal.
(c) Retrieval.

3 The brief duration, limited capacity store is:
(a) SLR.
(b) STM.
(c) LTM.

4 Coding in LTM is mostly:
(a) Acoustic.
(b) Semantic.
(c) Visual.

5 Patient KF had:
(a) More than one type of STM.
(b) More than one type of LTM.
(c) No functioning STM.

6 Craik and Watkins argue LTM storage requires:
(a) Nothing – it's automatic.
(b) Maintenance rehearsal.
(c) Elaborative rehearsal.

7 A major limitation of supporting studies is they:
(a) Are few and far between.
(b) Are conducted in real life.
(c) Use artificial materials.

8 There are different types of LTM, this:
(a) Supports the MSM.
(b) Challenges the MSM.
(c) Is irrelevant to the MSM.

Answers
1A 2A 3B 4B
5A 6C 7C 8B

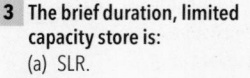

Possible extended writing questions:

• Outline and evaluate the multi-store model of memory. *[AS = 12, AL =16]*

• Discuss short-term memory **and** long-term memory. *[AS =12, AL = 16]*

Y1/AS Student Book
Pages 50–51

Y1/AS Revision Guide
Pages 34–35

Episodic memory

Memories of events, e.g. what you had for lunch.

Complex memories, time-stamped, conscious recall, about people and places.

Semantic memory

Knowledge of world ('facts'), e.g. what words mean.

Not time-stamped, less personal, shared knowledge.

Spec Spotlight

Types of long-term memory: episodic, semantic, procedural.

Procedural memory

Actions and skills, e.g. ride bike, how to 'do' things.

Recall without awareness or effort, hard to explain, automatic recall with practice.

(+) Case study support – in HM and Clive Wearing only one type of LTM damaged.

(+) Brain scan support – episodic in right prefrontal cortex and semantic in left (Tulving *et al.*).

(+) Real-life application – different types of LTM targeted to improve memory.

(−) Clinical evidence problems – amnesia cases (HM) lack control, findings hard to generalise.

(−) Two types of LTM not three – declarative and non-declarative (Cohen and Squire).

Topic 2: MEMORY

1 Episodic memories are:
(a) Impersonal.
(b) Time-stamped.
(c) Memories for facts.

2 Knowledge of word meanings is:
(a) Episodic.
(b) Semantic.
(c) Procedural.

3 Memories for actions are:
(a) Episodic.
(b) Semantic.
(c) Procedural.

4 Procedural memories are:
(a) Memories for events.
(b) Recalled automatically.
(c) Like a diary.

5 Studies of HM and Clive Wearing are:
(a) Case studies.
(b) Lab experiments.
(c) Field experiments.

6 Tulving found semantic memories stored in the:
(a) Left prefrontal cortex.
(b) Right prefrontal cortex.
(c) Cerebellum.

7 Studies of amnesia:
(a) Are highly reliable.
(b) Are highly generalisable.
(c) Lack control.

8 Declarative memory is:
(a) Procedural.
(b) Procedural and episodic.
(c) Episodic and semantic.

Answers
1B 2B 3C 4B
5A 6A 7C 8C

Topic 2: MEMORY

Possible extended writing questions:

- Describe and evaluate research into **at least two** types of long-term memory. *[AS =12, AL = 16]*
- Outline and evaluate research into types of long-term memory. Refer in your answer to episodic, semantic **and** procedural memories. *[AS =12, AL = 16]*

Topic 2: MEMORY

Spec Spotlight

The working memory model: central executive, phonological loop, visuo-spatial sketchpad and episodic buffer. Features of the model: coding and capacity.

WMM is a model of STM, its structure and function – four key components.

Central executive (CE) – very limited *capacity*, allocates subsystems/resources to tasks.

Phonological loop (PL) – auditory *coding*:
- Phonological store holds words heard.
- Articulatory process allows rehearsal.
- *Capacity* is about two seconds of what you can say.

Visuo-spatial sketchpad – visual/spatial *coding*:
- Visual cache stores visual data.
- Inner scribe records objects in vision.
- *Capacity* is three or four objects.

Episodic buffer – integrates data from other stores, time-sequencing, links to LTM.

(+) Support from KF – separate acoustic and visual stores (Shallice and Warrington).

(+) Dual task studies – poor performance on two visual tasks, shows existence of VSS.

(−) Central executive unclear – vague and may have several components.

(+) Word length effect – supports limited articulatory process in PL (Baddeley).

(+) Support from brain scans – CE may be in prefrontal cortex (Braver *et al.*).

1 WMM is a model of:
(a) Function of STM.
(b) Structure of LTM.
(c) Organisation of sensory register.

2 The central executive:
(a) Allocates subsystems to tasks.
(b) Has unlimited capacity.
(c) Stores visual information.

3 The articulatory process:
(a) Is part of the VSS.
(b) Stores words.
(c) Allows rehearsal.

4 The subsystem linked to LTM is:
(a) The phonological loop.
(b) The episodic buffer.
(c) The visuo-spatial sketchpad.

5 KF had:
(a) No LTM.
(b) Two separate STM stores.
(c) Just visual STM.

6 Existence of the VSS is shown by:
(a) Dual-task performance studies.
(b) The word length effect.
(c) Brain scan studies.

7 The central executive is:
(a) Very well understood.
(b) Vaguely defined.
(c) A minor part of the WMM.

8 Brain scans suggest the CE is:
(a) Part of the PL.
(b) In the prefrontal cortex.
(c) Not physically part of the brain.

Answers
1A 2A 3C 4B
5B 6A 7B 8B

Possible extended writing questions:

- Outline and evaluate the working memory model. *[AS =12, AL = 16]*
- Discuss research into the working memory model. Refer to **both** coding **and** capacity. *[AS =12, AL = 16]*
- Discuss the working memory model. In your answer refer to the multi-store model. *[AS =12, AL = 16]*

A01 | **Explanations for forgetting: Interference** | **A03**

Interference

Forgetting occurs when two pieces of information conflict.

Proactive interference – older memory disrupts a newer one.

Retroactive interference – newer memory disrupts an older one.

Both types of interference are worse when the memories are similar.

Key study: McGeoch and McDonald

Procedure – participants learned two lists of items, 6 conditions, e.g. synonyms.

Finding – recall of 1st list worse when 2nd list similar.

⊕ Lab studies – many controlled experiments demonstrate interference.

⊖ Artificial materials – less interference in real-life forgetting than in the lab.

⊕ Real-life support for interference – e.g. rugby players (Baddeley and Hitch).

⊖ Time between learning and recall – much less in lab studies than in real life.

⊖ Cues can remove interference effects – memories become accessible (Tulving and Psotka).

Spec Spotlight

Explanations for forgetting: proactive and retroactive interference.

Topic 2: MEMORY

1 Older memories disrupting newer ones is:
(a) Proactive interference.
(b) Projective interference.
(c) Retroactive interference.

2 The word 'synonyms' means words that have the:
(a) Same meaning.
(b) Different meanings.
(c) Adjectives.

3 How many IV conditions did McGeoch and McDonald use?
(a) 4
(b) 5
(c) 6

4 Which list caused most interference in this study?
(a) Nonsense syllables.
(b) Numbers.
(c) Synonyms.

5 Interference occurs most often in:
(a) Real life.
(b) Lab studies.
(c) Questionnaire studies.

6 Which study supports interference in real life?
(a) McGeoch and McDonald.
(b) Baddeley and Hitch.
(c) Tulving and Psotka.

7 Interference in the lab is exaggerated because:
(a) Real-life materials are used.
(b) Learning-recall interval is short.
(c) Variables are uncontrolled.

8 What did Tulving and Psotka use to challenge interference?
(a) Cues.
(b) Amnesic patients.
(c) Rugby players.

Topic 2: MEMORY

Answers
1A 2A 3C 4C
5B 6B 7B 8A

Possible extended writing questions:

- Discuss **one** explanation for forgetting. *[AS =12, AL = 16]*
- Describe and evaluate interference as an explanation for forgetting. *[AS =12, AL = 16]*

Explanations for forgetting: Retrieval failure

AO1 **AO3**

Y1/AS Student Book
Pages 56–57

Y1/AS Revision Guide
Pages 40–41

Retrieval failure due to absence of cues

Cues stored at same time as memory, cues help access memory.

Encoding specificity principle (ESP) – same cues at coding and retrieval aid recall (Tulving).

Some cues linked meaningfully – e.g. the letters 'STM' trigger recall of information.

Some cues not linked meaningfully – e.g. context information or emotional state.

Key study: Godden and Baddeley

Procedure – divers learned/recalled words in same/different context (land/water).

Finding – recall best when context at learning and recall matched.

⊕ Research evidence – many studies support theory (Godden and Baddeley).

⊖ Real-life context effect weak – contexts of learning/ recall not different enough.

⊖ Effect depends on testing – no context effects with recognition test (Godden and Baddeley).

⊖ ESP not testable – cannot independently establish cue is encoded.

⊕ Real-life application – context cues useful in real life (e.g. cognitive interview).

Spec Spotlight

Explanations for forgetting: retrieval failure due to absence of cues.

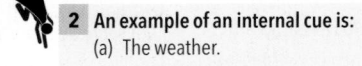

1 A retrieval cue is:
   (a) Used by snooker players.
   (b) Anything that triggers recall.
   (c) Always present at recall.

2 An example of an internal cue is:
   (a) The weather.
   (b) A specific place.
   (c) Feeling upset.

3 Godden and Baddeley's study involved:
   (a) Pool players.
   (b) Astronauts.
   (c) Deep-sea divers.

4 Recall was best when:
   (a) Learning and recall contexts matched.
   (b) Learning took place on land.
   (c) Learning took place underwater.

5 Context effects are:
   (a) Non-existent in lab studies.
   (b) Not supported by evidence.
   (c) Not very strong in real life.

6 Using recognition tests instead of recall, context effects:
   (a) Are stronger.
   (b) Are no different.
   (c) Disappear.

7 The problem with cues is:
   (a) There is only one type.
   (b) They cannot be measured independently of recall.
   (c) They cannot be studied.

8 One application of cues is:
   (a) Circular reasoning.
   (b) The cognitive interview.
   (c) Intelligence tests.

Topic 2: MEMORY

Answers
1B 2C 3C 4A
5C 6C 7B 8B

Possible extended writing questions:

- Outline and evaluate **two** explanations for forgetting. *[AS =12, AL = 16]*
- Discuss retrieval-failure due to absence of cues as an explanation for forgetting. *[AS =12, AL = 16]*

Spec Spotlight

Factors affecting the accuracy of eyewitness testimony: misleading information including leading questions and post-event Discussion.

Leading questions

Leading questions – question wording can distort memory/influence answer.

Loftus and Palmer – procedure, speed of car with different verbs ('smashed').

Findings – 31.8mph for 'contacted', 40.5 for 'smashed'.

Post-event Discussion

Discussing event afterwards could distort recall.

Gabbert *et al.* – procedure, pairs watched crime video, then discussed.

Findings – 71% wrongly recalled things they had discussed but not seen.

⊕ Real-life – application to understanding EWT, useful for police, courts.

⊖ Artificial tasks – watching film of incident less stressful than real life.

⊖ Individual differences in accuracy – not accounted for in studies (e.g. age).

⊖ Lab studies create demand characteristics – reduce validity of EWT research.

⊖ Low external validity – most EWT studies have no consequences for inaccuracy, unlike real life.

Topic 2: MEMORY

1 Leading questions:
(a) Improve witness recall.
(b) Can distort witness recall.
(c) Have no effect on witness recall.

2 Which verbs did Loftus and Palmer use?
(a) Smashed and crashed.
(b) Contacted and smashed.
(c) Crashed and hit.

3 Average response to 'smashed' was:
(a) 20.5 mph.
(b) 31.8 mph.
(c) 40.5 mph.

4 Post-event discussion was studied by:
(a) Yuille and Cutshall.
(b) Anastasi and Rhodes.
(c) Gabbert *et al.*

5 A major strength of EWT research is:
(a) Applications for the police.
(b) The materials used.
(c) External validity.

6 Watching film clips of car crashes in a lab is:
(a) An artificial task.
(b) More stressful than real life.
(c) Time-consuming.

7 Demand characteristics:
(a) Increase generalisability.
(b) Reduce a study's validity.
(c) Increase a study's reliability.

8 The consequences of inaccurate EWT in studies are:
(a) Very serious.
(b) Non-existent.
(c) Well-controlled.

Topic 2: MEMORY

Answers
1B 2B 3C 4C
5A 6A 7B 8B

Possible extended writing questions:

- Discuss **one** factor affecting the accuracy of eyewitness testimony. *[AS =12, AL = 16]*
- Outline and evaluate research into misleading information as a factor affecting the accuracy of eyewitness testimony. *[AS =12, AL = 16]*

Eyewitness testimony: Anxiety

Key study: Johnson and Scott

Procedure – heard argument, saw man with knife or pen.

Findings – high anxiety participants poor recall (weapon focus).

Key study: Yuille and Cutshall

Procedure – interviewed witnesses to real-life robbery.

Findings – high stress witnesses most accurate 5 months later.

Explaining contradictory results

Curvilinear relationship between stress and performance (inverted-U).

Deffenbacher – low/high anxiety poor recall, but moderate anxiety good recall.

$\ominus$ Weapon focus effect due to surprise – not anxiety (Pickel).

$\ominus$ Field studies lack control – so extraneous variables affect findings.

$\ominus$ Ethical issues – creating anxiety in participants, not true for real-life studies.

$\ominus$ Inverted-U theory simplistic – focuses only on physiology, so limited.

$\ominus$ Demand characteristics in lab studies – watching a film leads to expectations of questions later.

Spec Spotlight

Factors affecting the accuracy of eyewitness testimony: anxiety.

Topic 2: MEMORY

1 Johnson and Scott investigated:
(a) The weapons effect.
(b) Real-life EWT.
(c) The inverted-U theory.

2 In this study, participants in high anxiety condition (compared to low anxiety) had:
(a) Poorer face recognition.
(b) Better face recognition.
(c) The same face recognition.

3 Yuille and Cutshall's study:
(a) Was a lab experiment.
(b) Was a natural experiment.
(c) Was a field experiment.

4 The relationship between anxiety and accuracy is probably:
(a) Linear.
(b) A negative correlation.
(c) An inverted-U.

5 Pickel found poor recall was due to:
(a) Weapons effect.
(b) Anxiety.
(c) Surprise.

6 Creating anxiety in a lab study:
(a) Generalises well to real life.
(b) Is unethical.
(c) Is high in external validity.

7 Inverted-U theory is limited because it:
(a) Has demand characteristics.
(b) Focuses only on physiology.
(c) Does not address physiology.

8 Lab studies have demand characteristics because:
(a) Participants try to give 'helpful' answers.
(b) Of confounding variables.
(c) They are unethical.

Topic 2: MEMORY

Answers
1A 2A 3B 4C
5C 6B 7B 8A

Possible extended writing questions:
- Discuss **two** factors affecting the accuracy of eyewitness testimony. *[AS =12, AL = 16]*
- Outline and evaluate anxiety as a factor affecting the accuracy of eyewitness testimony. *[AS =12, AL = 16]*

AO1 Eyewitness testimony: Cognitive interview (CI) AO3

Fisher and Geiselman – CI based on psychological insights into memory.

Report everything – recall every detail even if trivial, could cue more recall.

Reinstate context – mentally return to original scene, context-dependent cue.

Reverse order – recall events backwards (or other order) to avoid expectations.

Change perspective – recall from another person's point of view.

Enhanced CI

More elements, e.g. reduce anxiety, open questions, speak slowly.

⊕ Some elements of CI useful – supported by research (Milne and Bull).

⊕ Support for enhanced CI – recall more accurate than standard interview (Köhnken et al.).

⊖ Time-consuming – full version of CI also requires training, so police reluctant.

⊖ Unreliable research – hard to compare studies using different versions of CI.

⊖ CI increases inaccurate recall as well as accuracy (Köhnken et al.).

Spec Spotlight

Improving the accuracy of eyewitness testimony including the use of the cognitive interview.

Eyewitness testimony: Cognitive interview – multiple choice questions

1 Reporting everything helps to:
(a) Ignore trivial details.
(b) See a different point of view.
(c) Cue further recall.

2 Mentally returning to the scene is:
(a) Changing the perspective.
(b) Reversing the order.
(c) Reinstating the context.

3 Influence of expectations can be avoided by:
(a) Reversing the order.
(b) Recalling everything.
(c) Reinstating the context.

4 Anxiety reduction is a feature of the:
(a) Standard police interview.
(b) Standard CI.
(c) Enhanced CI.

5 The best element of CI is:
(a) Report everything and reinstate context combined.
(b) Change perspective.
(c) Reverse the order.

6 Köhnken et al. found CI:
(a) Is only good for some witnesses.
(b) Increases amount of incorrect information.
(c) Is the same as the standard interview.

7 Police are reluctant to use CI because:
(a) It is too quick.
(b) It requires a lot of training.
(c) They know it doesn't work.

8 Studies into CI are unreliable because:
(a) Accuracy cannot be measured.
(b) They are poorly controlled.
(c) Different versions are used.

Topic 2: MEMORY

Answers
1C 2C 3A 4C
5A 6B 7B 8C

Possible extended writing questions:

- Outline and evaluate research into **one** way of improving the accuracy of eyewitness testimony. *[AS =12, AL = 16]*
- Discuss the cognitive interview in the context of improving the accuracy of eyewitness testimony. *[AS =12, AL = 16]*

Book-link

Y1/AS Student Book
Pages 74–75

Y1/AS Revision Guide
Pages 48–49

Babies have 'alert phases' – signal when they are ready for interaction.

Interactional synchrony

Baby and mother mirror actions and emotions.

Observation of adult and baby synchrony at two weeks (Meltzoff and Moore).

Important for attachment – higher synchrony linked to quality attachment.

Reciprocity

One person responds to other (a 'dance'), from 3 months.

Baby takes active role – can initiate interactions and take turns.

⊖ Hard to investigate infant behaviour – can't tell if behaviours have meaning.

⊕ Well-controlled procedures – e.g. interactions filmed, good validity.

⊖ Purpose of synchrony and reciprocity not considered (Feldman).

⊖ Socially sensitive research – implications for mothers returning to work.

⊕ Value to society – could use to improve mother–infant interactions in at-risk groups.

Spec Spotlight

Caregiver–infant interactions in humans: reciprocity and interactional synchrony.

Caregiver–infant interactions – multiple choice questions

1 Babies signal their readiness for interaction:
(a) All the time.
(b) Only when they are fed.
(c) In alert phases.

2 Infant and mother 'mirroring' is:
(a) Interactional synchrony.
(b) Interpersonal synchrony.
(c) Intergalactic synchrony.

3 Synchrony at two weeks was studied by:
(a) Hatzoff and Moore.
(b) Clozeoff and Moore.
(c) Meltzoff and Moore.

4 Reciprocity has been described as like a:
(a) Football match.
(b) Dance.
(c) Film.

5 5. Well-controlled procedures:
(a) Increase validity.
(b) Do not exist in this area of research.
(c) Have no effect on validity.

6 Observing synchrony and reciprocity does _not_:
(a) Have real-life application.
(b) Make any sense.
(c) Tell us what they are for.

7 Mothers who return to work:
(a) Benefit from reciprocity.
(b) May restrict opportunities for interactional synchrony.
(c) Must have training.

8 Improving mother–infant interactions is:
(a) An ethical issue.
(b) A waste of time.
(c) Valuable to society.

Answers
1C 2A 3C 4B
5A 6C 7B 8C

Possible extended writing questions:

- Discuss research into caregiver–infant interactions in humans. *[AS = 12, AL = 16]*
- In the context of caregiver–infant interactions, outline and evaluate reciprocity **and/or** interactional synchrony. *[AS = 12, AL = 16]*

Y1/AS Student Book
Pages 74–75
Y1/AS Revision Guide
Pages 50–51

Spec Spotlight

The role of the father.

Father primary attachment object in just 3% of cases (Schaffer and Emerson).

Secondary attachment formed with father within 18 months (75% of cases).

Infant–mother attachment more crucial in later teen attachments (Grossman).

Quality of fathers' play with infants linked to attachments – different role.

Fathers can be primary caregivers – adopt behaviours typical of mothers (Field).

Key to attachment is responsiveness of adult (e.g. smiling) not gender.

⊖ Research questions – researchers address different issues on fathers' role.

⊖ No distinct role – children without 2nd parent develop no differently so secondary attachment unimportant.

⊖ Fathers and primary attachments – hormones may predispose women to be nurturing.

⊖ Observations are biased – may be influenced by gender stereotypes.

⊕ Economic implications – mothers may feel freer to return to work and leave fathers at home.

Topic 3: ATTACHMENT

1 Schaffer and Emerson found fathers were main attachment figures in:
(a) 1% of cases.
(b) 3% of cases.
(c) 10% of cases.

2 A father's main role in children's lives may involve:
(a) Play and stimulation.
(b) Nurturing and caring.
(c) Going out to work.

3 When fathers are primary caregivers:
(a) They adopt maternal behaviours.
(b) They become more masculine.
(c) The baby is disadvantaged.

4 The key to successful attachment is being:
(a) Genetically related.
(b) Female.
(c) Responsive.

5 Children growing up in families with one parent develop:
(a) Abnormally.
(b) Slowly.
(c) No differently from other children.

6 Secondary attachments formed with father by:
(a) 6 months.
(b) 12 months.
(c) 18 months.

7 Biased observers:
(a) See what they expect to see.
(b) Record observations objectively.
(c) Do not exist in attachment research.

8 High quality attachment during teenage years most associated with:
(a) Attachment to mother.
(b) Attachment to father.
(c) Attachment to both parents.

Answers
1B 2A 3A 4C
5C 6C 7A 8A

Possible extended writing questions:
- Describe and evaluate the role of the father. Refer to research in your answer. *[AS = 12, AL = 16]*
- Discuss the role of the father in the context of multiple attachments. *[AS = 12, AL = 16]*

Book-link

Y1/AS Student Book
Pages 76–77

Y1/AS Revision Guide
Pages 52–53

Spec Spotlight

Stages of attachment as identified by Schaffer. Multiple attachments.

Stages of attachment

Asocial – first few weeks, baby behaves in same way to humans and objects.

Indiscriminate – preference for (familiar) people, no stranger/separation anxiety.

Specific – at about 7 months with one primary attachment figure.

Multiple attachments – by 12 months most babies form several more attachments.

Key study: Schaffer and Emerson

Procedure – 60 Glasgow babies observed at home by mothers.

Finding – 50% formed one attachment between 25 and 32 weeks, usually mother.

⊖ Difficult to assess multiple attachments – infant distress does not signify attachment.

⊖ Hard to study asocial babies – poor co-ordination, so just may seem asocial.

⊖ Conflicting evidence – multiple attachments appear earlier in collectivist cultures, i.e. not universal.

⊕ High external validity – parents did the observing so behaviour was natural.

⊕ Longitudinal/repeated measures – so no participant variables, high internal validity.

Schaffer's stages of attachment – multiple choice questions

1 Schaffer and Emerson's first stage is:
(a) Asocial.
(b) Multiple attachments.
(c) Indiscriminate attachments.

2 Separation anxiety appears in the:
(a) Indiscriminate attachment stage.
(b) Multiple attachments stage.
(c) Specific attachment stage.

3 Most babies form multiple attachments by:
(a) 12 months.
(b) 6 months.
(c) 3 months.

4 In Schaffer and Emerson's study the observations were:
(a) Made by researchers.
(b) Made by the babies' parents.
(c) Recorded using CCTV.

5 The most difficult stage to study is:
(a) Specific attachment.
(b) Multiple attachments.
(c) Asocial.

6 Multiple attachments appear relatively early in:
(a) Individualist cultures.
(b) Collectivist cultures.
(c) It is the same in all cultures.

7 Absence of observers meant Schaffer and Emerson's study:
(a) Had high internal validity.
(b) Had high external validity.
(c) Was very reliable.

8 In a longitudinal design:
(a) Participant variables are controlled.
(b) Situational variables are controlled.
(c) There is no independent variable.

Answers
1A 2C 3A 4B
5C 6B 7B 8A

Possible extended writing questions:
- Describe and evaluate the stages of attachment as identified by Schaffer. *[AS = 12, AL = 16]*
- Discuss research into stages of attachment. Refer to multiple attachments in your answer. *[AS = 12, AL = 16]*

AO1 **AO3**

Topic 3: ATTACHMENT

Book-link

Y1/AS Student Book
Pages 78–79

Y1/AS Revision Guide
Pages 54–55

Spec Spotlight

Animal studies
of attachment:
Lorenz and Harlow.

Key study: Lorenz

Procedure – 12 goose eggs, half saw mother within hours of hatching, half saw Lorenz.

Findings – goslings followed whichever was the first moving object they saw.

Conclusion – imprinting occurs in critical period, no attachment if outside that time.

⊖ Generalising birds to humans doubtful – attachment systems quite different.

⊕ Supporting evidence – chicks imprinted on washing-up gloves (Guiton).

⊖ Questionning Lorenz's conclusions – the imprinting didn't affect goslings later.

Key study: Harlow

Procedure – 16 infant rhesus monkeys raised with 'surrogate mothers'.

Findings – infants preferred cloth-covered mother to wire one with milk.

Conclusion – contact comfort more important than food in attachment.

⊕ Real-life application – showed importance of attachment (e.g. abuse).

⊖ Ethical issues – suffering of infant monkeys (but balance against benefits).

⊖ Generalising monkeys to humans – human communication influences attachment.

Animal studies of attachment — multiple choice questions

1 Lorenz studied:
(a) Attachment in humans.
(b) Imprinting in goslings.
(c) Maternal deprivation in monkeys.

2 The critical period for imprinting was:
(a) The first year.
(b) A few hours after hatching.
(c) Between 5 and 6 days.

3 Harlow's study used:
(a) Wire and cloth surrogate mothers.
(b) Washing-up gloves.
(c) Newly-hatched geese.

4 Harlow's monkeys preferred:
(a) Provision of food.
(b) Wire mothers.
(c) Contact comfort.

5 Lorenz's findings:
(a) Cannot explain imprinting.
(b) Are hard to generalise to humans.
(c) Were not the result of learning.

6 Lorenz's findings are challenged by:
(a) Guiton.
(b) Harlow.
(c) The goslings' later development.

7 An ethical issue in Harlow's study is:
(a) Deception.
(b) Lack of confidentiality.
(c) Psychological harm to the monkeys.

8 Harlow's findings:
(a) Account for the role of communication.
(b) Are easier to generalise to humans than Lorenz's.
(c) Are not applicable today.

Answers
1B 2B 3A 4C
5B 6C 7C 8B

Possible extended writing questions:

- Outline and evaluate animal studies of attachment. Refer to **two or more** studies in your answer. [AS = 12, AL = 16]
- Discuss animal studies of attachment by Lorenz **and/or** Harlow. [AS = 12, AL = 16]

AO1 | AO3

Book-link

Y1/AS Student Book
Pages 80–81

Y1/AS Revision Guide
Pages 56–57

Spec Spotlight

Explanations of
attachment:
learning theory.

Importance of food (Dollard and Miller) –
cupboard love, children learn to love whoever
provides food.

Classical conditioning – UCS (food) produces
UCR (feeling of pleasure).

Caregiver (NS) associated with food becomes CS,
produces pleasure (CR).

Operant conditioning – crying reinforced
because produces caregiver response.

Negative reinforcement – caregiver's response
reinforced because crying stops.

Drive reduction – attachment is secondary drive
learned by association of caregiver with hunger
satisfaction.

⊖ Animal studies – attachment does not
depend on feeding (Lorenz/Harlow).

⊖ Human studies – primary attachment
figure not always person who feeds
(Schaffer and Emerson).

⊖ Ignores other factors – food less
important than responsiveness, etc.

⊕ Some elements of conditioning are
involved – comfort/ interaction rather
than food.

⊖ Ignores social learning theory –
parents model attachment and reward
child.

Topic 3: ATTACHMENT

1 Learning theory is also called:
(a) Bowlby's theory.
(b) Evolutionary theory.
(c) Cupboard love theory.

2 Learning through association is:
(a) Classical conditioning.
(b) Operant conditioning.
(c) Negative reinforcement.

3 Food is the:
(a) UCR.
(b) CS.
(c) UCS.

4 A caregiver stopping a baby's crying receives:
(a) Drive reduction.
(b) Negative reinforcement.
(c) Classical conditioning.

5 Learning theory of attachment is challenged by:
(a) Animal studies.
(b) Classical conditioning.
(c) Operant conditioning.

6 In humans, the main attachment figure:
(a) Is the unconditioned response.
(b) Provides negative reinforcement.
(c) Does not always provide food.

7 Food is less important than:
(a) The unconditioned stimulus.
(b) An innate biological motivator.
(c) The caregiver's responsiveness.

8 A newer learning explanation is:
(a) Modelling.
(b) Drive reduction.
(c) Reinforcement.

Topic 3: ATTACHMENT

Answers
1C 2A 3C 4B
5A 6C 7C 8A

Possible extended writing questions:

- Discuss **one** explanation of attachment. *[AS = 12, AL = 16]*
- Outline and evaluate learning theory as an explanation of attachment. *[AS = 12, AL = 16]*

Attachment is innate – evolutionary survival advantage (e.g. imprinting).

Monotropic – attachment to primary figure, is different and special.

Time spent with mother-figure – beneficial because law of continuity and law of accumulated separation.

Social releasers – innate cute behaviours activate attachment in adults.

Critical period – no attachment in first 2 years makes it harder to form later.

Internal working model (IWM) – first attachment is template for later relationships.

⊖ Mixed evidence for monotropy – many babies form multiple attachments early.

⊕ Evidence for social releasers – babies distressed when 'cute' signals ignored.

⊕ Evidence for IWM – poor attachment passed on in families (Bailey *et al.*).

⊖ Socially sensitive research – mothers blamed for spending time away from children.

⊖ Wrong emphasis – baby's temperament may explain social behaviour more than attachment.

Spec Spotlight

Explanations of attachment: Bowlby's monotropic theory. The concepts of a critical period and an internal working model.

Topic 3: ATTACHMENT

1 A caregiver–infant attachment:
(a) Has no real benefits.
(b) Is based on food.
(c) Gives a survival advantage.

2 A special attachment to one person is called:
(a) Ditropic.
(b) Monotropic.
(c) Bitropic.

3 One of Bowlby's 'laws' is the law of:
(a) Primary attachment.
(b) Accumulated separation.
(c) Critical period.

4 A baby's innate 'cute' behaviours:
(a) Are learned.
(b) Produce no response from adults.
(c) Are called social releasers.

5 Evidence for monotropy is mixed because:
(a) Many babies form multiple attachments early on.
(b) Most babies do not form a specific attachment.
(c) Some babies attach to fathers.

6 The internal working model was investigated by:
(a) Schaffer and Emerson.
(b) Bailey et al.
(c) Brazleton et al.

7 The concept of monotropy is considered:
(a) Socially sensitive.
(b) Invalid nowadays.
(c) Outdated.

8 What may be more important than attachment in social behaviour?
(a) Baby's temperament.
(b) Parent's personality.
(c) Parent's income.

Answers
1C 2B 3B 4C
5A 6B 7A 8A

Possible extended writing questions:
- Describe and evaluate **two** explanations of attachment. *[AS = 12, AL = 16]*
- Discuss Bowlby's monotropic theory of attachment. Refer in your answer to the concepts of critical period **and** internal working model. *[AS = 12, AL = 16]*

Book-link

Y1/AS Student Book
Pages 84–85

Y1/AS Revision Guide
Pages 60–61

Spec Spotlight

Ainsworth's
Strange Situation.
Types of attachment:
secure, insecure-avoidant
and insecure-resistant.

Procedure

Controlled observation in lab – assess quality of caregiver–infant attachment.

Five categories used – including proximity-seeking, separation anxiety.

Seven episodes (3 mins), e.g. stranger enters, caregiver leaves, stranger returns.

Findings – Three types of attachment

Secure (60–75% of British toddlers) – secure base/moderate anxiety.

Insecure-avoidant (20–25%) – no secure base, no stranger/separation anxiety.

Insecure-resistant (3%) – extreme anxiety, resist comfort on reunion with caregiver.

$\oplus$ High predictive validity – attachment type linked to later outcomes.

$\oplus$ Good inter-rater reliability – 94% observers agree on attachment type (Bick).

$\ominus$ Culture-bound test – Strange Situation behaviours different meanings outside US/Europe.

$\ominus$ Confounding variable – role of temperament more important influence than attachment quality/type.

$\ominus$ Other attachment types – e.g. disorganised, questions validity of Strange Situation classification.

Topic 3: ATTACHMENT

1 The Strange Situation is:
(a) A controlled lab-based observation.
(b) Interview-based.
(c) A questionnaire method.

2 The Strange Situation includes:
(a) 7 categories, 5 episodes.
(b) 5 categories, 5 episodes.
(c) 5 categories, 7 episodes.

3 60–75% of attachments in Ainsworth's study were:
(a) Insecure-avoidant.
(b) Insecure-resistant.
(c) Secure.

4 Moderate stranger anxiety is a sign of:
(a) An insecure attachment.
(b) A secure attachment.
(c) A disorganised attachment.

5 Link between attachment type and later outcomes shows the Strange Situation:
(a) Has predictive validity.
(b) Is unreliable.
(c) Lacks validity.

6 Bick found inter-rater reliability in the Strange Situation of:
(a) 76%
(b) 84%
(c) 94%

7 One problem with the Strange Situation is that it is:
(a) Culture-bound.
(b) Conducted in people's homes.
(c) Not relevant today.

8 There is another attachment type called:
(a) Disinterested.
(b) Organised.
(c) Disorganised.

Answers
1A 2C 3C 4B
5A 6C 7A 8C

Possible extended writing questions:
- Discuss Ainsworth's Strange Situation. *[AS = 12, AL = 16]*
- Describe and evaluate **two or more** types of attachment in the context of Ainsworth's Strange Situation. *[AS = 12, AL = 16]*

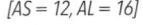

Book-link

Y1/AS Student Book
Pages 86–87

Y1/AS Revision Guide
Pages 62–63

AO1

Cultural variations in attachment

AO3

Key study: Van IJzendoorn and Kroonenberg

Procedure – meta-analysis of 32 studies using Strange Situation in several countries/cultures.

Findings – secure attachment most common (ranged from 50% China to 75% Britain).

Conclusion – more insecure-resistant type in collectivist cultures (e.g. Japan) than individualist (e.g. US).

Key study: Simonelli *et al.*

Procedure – Strange Situation used with 76 one year olds in Italy.

Findings – 50% secure (lower than previous studies), 36% insecure-avoidant.

Conclusion – change due to mothers working longer and using professional childcare.

$\oplus$ Meta-analyses – large sample sizes increase internal validity.

$\ominus$ Samples not representative of cultures – many cultural groups within a country.

$\ominus$ Cultural bias of Strange Situation – an imposed etic (favours US, UK), ignores cultural emic.

$\ominus$ Alternative explanation – cultural similarities in attachment types not innate but due to media.

$\ominus$ Temperament – more important influence in Strange Situation behaviour than attachment quality.

Spec Spotlight

Cultural variations in attachment including van IJzendoorn.

Topic 3: ATTACHMENT

1 Van IJzendoorn and Kroonenberg's study was a:
(a) Laboratory experiment.
(b) Meta-analysis.
(c) Questionnaire study.

2 In Van IJzendoorn and Kroonenberg's study the most common attachment type was:
(a) Insecure-resistant.
(b) Secure.
(c) Insecure-avoidant.

3 Simonelli et al. carried out their study in:
(a) Italy.
(b) The UK.
(c) The USA.

4 What proportion of insecure-avoidant type did Simonelli et al. find?
(a) 26%
(b) 50%
(c) 36%

5 A benefit of meta-analyses is that they:
(a) Are well controlled.
(b) Are quick and easy to do.
(c) Have large sample sizes.

6 The samples in van IJzendoorn and Kroonenberg's study were:
(a) Unrepresentative of cultures.
(b) Unrepresentative of countries.
(c) Unreliable.

7 The Strange Situation may be culturally biased towards:
(a) China and Japan.
(b) The US and UK.
(c) Europe.

8 Cultural similarities in attachment may be due to:
(a) Genetic factors.
(b) Media influences.
(c) Similar mothers.

Answers
1B 2B 3A 4C
5C 6A 7B 8B

Possible extended writing questions:

• Discuss cultural variations in attachment. *[AS = 12, AL = 16]*
• Outline and evaluate Van IJzendoorn's research into cultural variations in attachment. *[AS = 12, AL = 16]*

Bowlby's theory of maternal deprivation

Book-link

Y1/AS Student Book
Pages 88–89

Y1/AS Revision Guide
Pages 64–65

AO1

Continuous maternal care needed for healthy development.

Deprivation is loss of emotional care, negative effects if during first 30 months (critical period).

Intellectual – deprivation reduces IQ (Goldfarb, institutionalised children).

Emotional – leads to affectionless psychopathy (cannot experience guilt).

Key study: Bowlby

Procedure – interviewed 44 young thieves and families.

Findings – 14 affectionless psychopaths, 12 separated from mothers before 2 years of age.

AO3

⊖ Flawed evidence – e.g. Bowlby conducted interviews himself (bias).

⊖ Counter-evidence – fewer negative effects in bigger replication (Lewis).

⊖ Sensitive not critical period – Czech twins recovered from severe deprivation (Koluchová).

⊕ Animal studies support – deprivation has long-term effects in rats (Levy et al.).

⊖ Privation not deprivation – privation more damaging long term (Rutter).

Spec Spotlight

Bowlby's theory of maternal deprivation.

Bowlby's theory of maternal deprivation – multiple choice questions

1 For healthy development, maternal care must be:
(a) Provided by the mother.
(b) Provided by any female.
(c) Continuous.

2 The critical period for maternal deprivation is:
(a) 30 months.
(b) 24 months.
(c) 12 months.

3 One effect of maternal deprivation on intellectual development is:
(a) Reduction in IQ.
(b) Disinhibited attachment.
(c) Emotional harm.

4 Bowlby studied:
(a) 99 red balloons.
(b) 44 affectionless psychopaths.
(c) 44 juvenile thieves.

5 Strong support for Bowlby's theory comes from:
(a) Lewis's replication.
(b) Animal studies.
(c) Koluchová's study.

6 The Czech twins study shows that the critical period is in fact:
(a) A sensitive period.
(b) Non-existent.
(c) Shorter than Bowlby thought.

7 Rutter believed that Bowlby's study was actually about:
(a) Privation.
(b) Cultural variations.
(c) Types of attachment.

8 Bowlby's assessment of his participants was probably:
(a) Highly reliable.
(b) Biased.
(c) Objective.

Answers
1C 2A 3A 4C
5B 6A 7A 8B

Topic 3: ATTACHMENT

Possible extended writing questions:

- Outline and evaluate Bowlby's theory of maternal deprivation. *[AS = 12, AL = 16]*
- Discuss Bowlby's theories relating to attachment. *[AS = 12, AL = 16]*

AO1

AO3

Book-link

Y1/AS Student Book
Pages 90–91

Y1/AS Revision Guide
Pages 66–67

Effects of institutionalisation – disinhibited attachment and intellectual retardation.

Key study: Rutter et al.

Procedure – 165 Romanian orphans adopted in UK.

Findings – children adopted after 2 years had mean IQ of 77 at age 11.

Sensitive period – lack of attachment before 6 months has long-term effects (disinhibited attachment).

Key study: Zeanah et al.

Procedure – Strange Situation, assessed 95 institutionalised children.

Findings – only 19% secure attachment, 65% disorganised attachment type.

(+) Real-life application – improved caring in institutions (e.g. key workers for each child).

(+) Confounding variables – fewer in these studies because no early trauma.

(−) Generalisability issues – Romanian orphanages unusually poor care.

(−) Not randomly assigned – sociable babies might be adopted earlier (Rutter et al.).

(−) Long-term effects not yet clear – e.g. late-adopted children may 'catch up'.

Topic 3: ATTACHMENT

Spec Spotlight

Romanian orphan studies: effects of institutionalisation.

1 Rutter *et al.* studied:
(a) 165 adopted British children.
(b) 95 institutionalised Italian children.
(c) 165 Romanian orphans.

2 At 11 years, an average IQ of 77 was found for children adopted:
(a) After 2 years.
(b) Between 6 months and 2 years.
(c) Before 6 months.

3 The researchers found a sensitive period for attachments of:
(a) 6 months.
(b) 12 months.
(c) 24 months.

4 Zeanah *et al.* found disorganised attachment type in:
(a) 19% of all babies.
(b) 65% of institutionalised babies.
(c) 65% of all babies.

5 One real-life application of orphan research is:
(a) Children are not adopted early.
(b) Institutional care is improved.
(c) There are no more institutions.

6 One benefit of Romanian orphan studies (compared to older studies) is:
(a) Findings are easily generalised.
(b) Institutions are representative.
(c) They have fewer confounding variables.

7 *Not* randomly assigning babies to types of care may mean:
(a) Sociable babies are adopted earlier.
(b) Sociable babies are adopted later.
(c) Parents don't have a say in the babies adopted.

8 The long-term effects of early adoption are:
(a) Extremely serious.
(b) Currently unclear.
(c) Not as bad as first thought.

Answers
1C 2A 3A 4B
5B 6C 7A 8B

Possible extended writing questions:

- Describe and evaluate **two or more** Romanian orphan studies. *[AS = 12, AL = 16]*
- Outline and evaluate research into the effects of institutionalisation. *[AS = 12, AL = 16]*

Y1/AS Student Book
Pages 92–93

Y1/AS Revision Guide
Pages 68–69

Internal working model (IWM)

First attachment is template for future relationships.

Good early attachment – expect good later relationships (vice versa for bad).

Secure infants form better friendships and less likely to become bullies.

Parenting style based on IWM, so attachment type passed on in families.

Key study: Hazan and Shaver

Procedure – analysed 620 replies to a 'love quiz'.

Findings – 56% classed as secure (and had long lasting relationships), 25% insecure-avoidant (were jealous, feared intimacy).

⊖ Mixed evidence on continuity – no link between attachments in infancy and adolescence.

⊖ Validity issues – studies using self-report rely on accuracy and honesty.

⊖ Association not causation – intervening variable (e.g. temperament).

⊖ Exaggerates influence – attachments in infancy not that important later.

⊖ Theoretical problems – IWMs are unconscious, so should not be measurable by self-report.

Spec Spotlight

The influence of early attachment on childhood and adult relationships, including the role of an internal working model.

Topic 3: ATTACHMENT

1 First attachment is important because it:
- (a) Prevents deprivation.
- (b) Ensures a good marriage.
- (c) Is a template for future relationships.

2 Better friendships in childhood are formed by infants who had:
- (a) Insecure-resistant attachment.
- (b) Insecure-avoidant attachment.
- (c) Secure attachment.

3 Attachment type can be:
- (a) Inherited.
- (b) Passed on in families.
- (c) Different in boys and girls.

4 Hazan and Shaver found 25% of their respondents were:
- (a) Secure.
- (b) Insecure-resistant.
- (c) Insecure-avoidant.

5 Some studies lack validity because:
- (a) They rely on honest and accurate self-reports.
- (b) They are well controlled.
- (c) Observations are biased.

6 Many research studies into IWMs are:
- (a) Lab experiments.
- (b) Correlational.
- (c) Case studies.

7 The influence of attachments on later relationships:
- (a) May have been exaggerated.
- (b) Is greater than any other factor.
- (c) Is always negative.

8 If IWMs are unconscious this means they:
- (a) Should not be measurable by self-report.
- (b) Are repressed because they create anxiety.
- (c) Have no effect on behaviour.

Answers
1C 2C 3B
4C 5A 6B
7A 8A

Possible extended writing questions:

- Discuss the influence of early attachment on childhood **and/or** adult relationships. *[AS = 12, AL = 16]*
- Outline and evaluate research into the role of an internal working model in childhood **and** adult relationships. *[AS = 12, AL = 16]*

AO1 · AO3

Book Link

Y1/AS Student Book
Pages 134–135

Y1/AS Revision Guide
Pages 90–91

Spec Spotlight

Definitions of
abnormality,
including statistical
infrequency and
deviation from social
norms.

Topic 4: PSYCHOPATHOLOGY

Statistical infrequency

Define abnormality using numbers.

Behaviour that is statistically rare is abnormal.

E.g. intellectual disability disorder – 2% of
people have IQ below 70.

(+) Real-life application – intellectual
disability disorder.

(−) Unusual characteristics can also be
positive.

(−) Not everyone unusual benefits from a
label.

Deviation from social norms

Behaviour that goes against expectations.

Related to cultural and historical context.

E.g. antisocial personality disorder – person
who goes against ethical norms.

(−) Not a sole explanation for abnormality.

(−) Norms are culturally relative.

(−) Definition could lead to human rights
abuses.

Definitions of abnormality 1 – multiple choice questions

1 Defining rare behaviour as abnormal is:
(a) Statistical inaccuracy.
(b) Statistical infrequency.
(c) Statistical inadequacy.

2 Intellectual disability disorder is an IQ below:
(a) 70
(b) 60
(c) 50

3 What % of the population have intellectual disability disorder?
(a) 6
(b) 4
(c) 2

4 A strength of statistical infrequency is:
(a) It's the only plausible definition of abnormality.
(b) Rare behaviour is easy to define.
(c) Real-life application.

5 Behaviour that goes against expectations is:
(a) Deviation from special norms.
(b) Deviation from social norms.
(c) Deviation form spatial norms.

6 Deviation from social norms is not influenced by:
(a) Culture.
(b) Historical context.
(c) Biology.

7 A person who does not observe ethical norms has:
(a) Interpersonal sociability disorder.
(b) Antisocial personality disorder.
(c) Intellectual disability disorder.

8 Not a criticism of deviation from social norms:
(a) Norms are culturally relative.
(b) Rare characteristics can also be positive.
(c) Could lead to human rights abuses.

Answers
1B 2A 3C 4C
5B 6C 7B 8B

Possible extended writing questions:

• Discuss **at least one** definition(s) of abnormality. *[AS = 12, AL = 16]*
• Outline and evaluate statistical infrequency **and** deviation from social norms as definitions of abnormality. *[AS = 12, AL = 16]*

Failure to function adequately

Inability to cope with everyday living.

Examples of not coping – not conforming to interpersonal rules, personal distress, irrational/dangerous behaviour.

E.g. intellectual disability disorder – low IQ may mean person cannot cope.

⊕ Recognises patient's individual perspective.

⊖ Difficult to distinguish from deviation from social norms.

⊖ Based on subjective judgment by psychiatrist.

Deviation from ideal mental health

Define what makes someone 'normal'.

Jahoda listed criteria for mental health.

E.g. being rational, accurate perception of self, self-actualisation.

⊕ Covers broad range of criteria.

⊖ Biased towards individualist culture.

⊖ Sets unrealistic standard for mental health.

Spec Spotlight

Definitions of abnormality, including failure to function adequately and deviation from ideal mental health.

Topic 4: PSYCHOPATHOLOGY

1 **Inability to cope with everyday living:**
   (a) Failure to function satisfactorily.
   (b) Failure to function accurately.
   (c) Failure to function adequately.

2 ***Not* an example of an interpersonal rule:**
   (a) Maintaining physical fitness.
   (b) Taking turns in a conversation.
   (c) Maintaining personal space.

3 **Someone who is *not* functioning adequately is unlikely to behave:**
   (a) Irrationally.
   (b) Dangerously.
   (c) Predictably.

4 **A strength of the failure to function adequately definition is:**
   (a) Recognises patient's perspective.
   (b) It covers a broad range of criteria.
   (c) It's the only plausible definition of abnormality.

5 **Proposed criteria for ideal mental health:**
   (a) Jahola.
   (b) Jahova.
   (c) Jahoda.

6 **Realising one's potential is called:**
   (a) Self-perception.
   (b) Self-realisation.
   (c) Self-actualisation.

7 **Deviation from ideal mental health is best applied to:**
   (a) Individualist culture.
   (b) Collectivist culture.
   (c) Industrialised culture.

8 **A strength of the deviation from ideal mental health definition is:**
   (a) Jahoda's criteria are universal.
   (b) Covers broad range of criteria.
   (c) It sets a realistic standard for mental health.

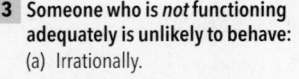

Answers
1C 2A 3C 4A
5C 6C 7A 8B

Possible extended writing questions:
- Discuss **two or more** definitions of abnormality. *[AS = 12, AL = 16]*
- Outline and evaluate failure to function adequately **and** deviation from ideal mental health as definitions of abnormality. *[AS = 12, AL = 16]*

Clinical characteristics of phobias, depression, OCD

A01　　　　　　　　　　　　　　　　　　　　　　**A01**

Book-link

Y1/AS Student Book
Pages 138–143

Y1/AS Revision Guide
Pages 94–95

Phobias	Behavioural	• Panic, such as screaming or running away. • Avoidance of phobic stimulus.
	Emotional	• Fear is immediate, leads to anxiety. • Response is disproportionate to threat.
	Cognitive	• Selective attention to the phobic stimulus. • Irrational beliefs, such as a tiny spider will kill me!
Depression	Behavioural	• Reduced energy levels, e.g. unable to get out of bed. • Avoidance of phobic stimulus.
	Emotional	• Poor concentration/difficulty making decisions. • Lowered mood, feelings of worthlessness.
	Cognitive	• Anger, leading to aggression or self-harm. • Absolutist thinking, unfortunate situations seen as disasters.
OCD	Behavioural	• Compulsions, ritually repeating behaviour, e.g. handwashing. • Avoidance of phobic stimulus
	Emotional	• Anxiety and distress which can be overwhelming. • Guilt and disgust, towards oneself or external stimuli, e.g. dirt.
	Cognitive	• Obsessive thoughts which are recurring and intrusive. • Insight into excessive anxiety, 'hypervigilance' (over-aware).

Spec Spotlight

The behavioural, emotional and cognitive characteristics of phobias, depression and obsessive-compulsive disorder (OCD).

1 *Not* a behavioural characteristic of phobias:
(a) Irrational beliefs.
(b) Panic.
(c) Avoidance.

2 A cognitive characteristic of phobias:
(a) Selective attention to the phobic stimulus.
(b) Anxiety.
(c) Panic.

3 Thinking a tiny spider will kill you is an example of:
(a) Avoidance.
(b) An irrational belief.
(c) Selective attention to phobic stimulus.

4 Self-harm is an example of:
(a) Action.
(b) Anxiety.
(c) Anger.

5 Inability to get out of bed is an example of:
(a) Absolutist thinking.
(b) Poor concentration.
(c) Reduced energy levels.

6 A cognitive characteristic of depression:
(a) Lowered mood.
(b) Anger.
(c) Absolutist thinking.

7 Repeatedly washing your hands is an example of:
(a) Hypervigilance.
(b) Compulsions.
(c) Obsessive thoughts.

8 Self-disgust is an example of:
(a) Behavioural characteristic of phobia.
(b) Emotional characteristic of OCD.
(c) Cognitive characteristic of depression.

Topic 4: PSYCHOPATHOLOGY

Answers
1A 2A 3B 4C
5C 6C 7B 8B

Possible questions:
- Identify **two** emotional characteristics of depression. *[AS and AL = 2]*
- Outline **one** behavioural and **one** cognitive characteristic of depression. *[AS and AL = 4]*
- Explain behavioural characteristics of OCD. *[AS and AL = 4]*

The behavioural approach to explaining phobias

AO1

AO3

Two-process model – phobias learned by classical, maintained by operant.

Classical conditioning – NS paired with CS causes CR (fear).

Little Albert conditioned to fear white rats.

Generalisation of fear to other stimuli.

Operant conditioning – avoiding phobia causes relief (negative reinforcement).

E.g. fear of clowns (coulrophobia) is maintained by relief from avoiding circuses.

$\oplus$ Application to therapy – phobia treated by preventing avoidance.

$\ominus$ Alternative explanations – e.g. in agoraphobia, safety motivates avoidance not reduction of anxiety.

$\ominus$ Incomplete – e.g. biological preparedness explains innate phobias

$\ominus$ Not all bad experiences lead to phobias – e.g. Di Nardo *et al.* (1988) dog study.

$\ominus$ Does not properly consider cognitive aspects of phobias.

Spec Spotlight

The behavioural approach to explaining phobias: the two-process model, including classical and operant conditioning.

Topic 4: PSYCHOPATHOLOGY

1 Phobias are learned by classical conditioning and maintained by:
- (a) Operative conditioning.
- (b) Operational conditioning.
- (c) Operant conditioning.

2 In classical conditioning:
- (a) NS is paired with UCS to produce CS and CR.
- (b) CS is paired with CR to produce UCS and NS.
- (c) NS is paired with CR to produce CS and UCS.

3 Conditioned to fear white rats:
- (a) Little Alfred.
- (b) Little Albert.
- (c) Little Alan.

4 When a phobia is applied to other similar stimuli:
- (a) Generalisation.
- (b) Specification.
- (c) Reproduction.

5 Coulrophobia is the fear of:
- (a) Clowns.
- (b) Clouds.
- (c) Clothes.

6 Suggests some phobias are innate:
- (a) Biological readiness.
- (b) Biological sensitiveness.
- (c) Biological preparedness.

7 Di Nardo found that *not* all those who had a bad experience developed a fear of:
- (a) The dentist.
- (b) The dark.
- (c) Dogs.

8 The two-process model does *not* properly consider:
- (a) Learned aspects of phobias.
- (b) Cognitive aspects of phobias.
- (c) How phobias are maintained.

Topic 4: PSYCHOPATHOLOGY

Answers
1C 2A 3B 4A
5A 6C 7C 8B

Possible extended writing questions:
- Discuss the two-process model of phobias. *[AS = 12, AL = 16]*
- Outline and evaluate the behavioural approach to explaining phobias. *[AS = 12, AL = 16]*

The behavioural approach to treating phobias

AO1 AO3

Systematic desensitisation (SD)

Counter-conditioning and reciprocal inhibition.

Anxiety hierarchy – feared stimuli from least to most frightening.

Relaxation techniques practised at each level (gradual exposure).

(+) Effective for spider phobics (Gilroy *et al.*).

(+) Suitable for diverse patients – e.g. with learning difficulties.

(+) More acceptable, less traumatic than flooding – low dropout rates.

Flooding

Immediate exposure to phobic stimulus.

Fear response is exhausted, phobia becomes extinct.

Ethical issues – patients must give informed consent and know what to expect.

(−) Less effective for social phobia.

(−) Traumatic – so time and money may be wasted.

(+) For some may be as effective and is quicker than SD.

Topic 4: PSYCHOPATHOLOGY

Spec Spotlight

The behavioural approach to treating phobias: systematic desensitisation including relaxation and use of a hierarchy; flooding.

The behavioural approach to treating phobias – multiple choice questions

1 The idea that fear and relaxation *cannot* occur together:
(a) Reciprocal exhibition.
(b) Reciprocal initiation.
(c) Reciprocal inhibition.

2 In systematic desensitisation, moving from least feared to most feared stimuli is the basis of:
(a) An anxiety hierarchy.
(b) A fear staircase.
(c) A trauma stepladder.

3 Relaxation techniques are unlikely to include:
(a) Deep breathing.
(b) Meditation.
(c) Smoking.

4 Flooding is based on:
(a) Gradual exposure.
(b) Immediate exposure.
(c) Minimal exposure.

5 In flooding, once the fear response is exhausted, the phobia is:
(a) Redundant.
(b) Extinct.
(c) Dormant.

6 Before flooding, patients must give:
(a) Consent.
(b) Concept.
(c) Contact.

7 Gilroy *et al.* gave systematic desensitisation to:
(a) Agoraphobics.
(b) Arachnophobics.
(c) Claustrophobics.

8 Which is true?
(a) Systematic desensitisation is more traumatic than flooding.
(b) Flooding is more traumatic than systematic desensitisation.
(c) Systematic desensitisation and flooding are equally traumatic.

Topic 4: PSYCHOPATHOLOGY

Answers
1C 2A 3C 4B
5B 6A 7B 8B

Possible extended writing questions:

- Outline and evaluate systematic desensitisation **and** flooding as treatments for phobias. *[AS = 12, AL = 16]*
- Discuss the behavioural approach to treating phobias. *[AS = 12, AL = 16]*

The cognitive approach to explaining depression

A01 **A03**

Topic 4: PSYCHOPATHOLOGY

Beck's negative triad

Depressives have faulty information processing.

Negative self-schema – interpret info about themselves in a negative way.

Negative triad – negative views of the world, the future, the self.

(+) Supporting evidence – pregnant women high in cognitive vulnerability had more post-natal depression (Grazioli and Terry).

(+) Real-life application – Beck's theory led to cognitive behaviour therapy (CBT).

(−) Beck's theory does not explain all aspects of depression – e.g. delusions.

Spec Spotlight

The cognitive approach to explaining depression: Beck's negative triad and Ellis' ABC model.

Ellis' ABC model

A for Activating event – e.g. the end of a relationship.

B for Beliefs – irrational beliefs, e.g. musterbation, 'I-can't-stand-it-itis'.

C for Consequence – e.g. failing a test triggers depression.

(−) Ellis' model, partial explanation – not all depression follows activating event.

(−) Cognitions may not be root cause of depression – emotions also important.

(+) Real-life application – this theory led to REBT.

1 *Not* part of the negative triad:
(a) Negative views of the self.
(b) Negative views of the world.
(c) Negative views of the past.

2 Introduced the ABC model:
(a) Beck.
(b) Ellis.
(c) Elbeck.

3 Which of the following is incorrect?
(a) A is for Anticipation.
(b) B is for Beliefs.
(c) C is for Consequence.

4 A form of irrational belief:
(a) I-don't-want-it-itis.
(b) I-can't-do-it-itis.
(c) I-can't-stand-it-itis.

5 Depressed people experience negative:
(a) Role schema.
(b) Person schema.
(c) Self-schema.

6 Grazioli and Terry studied:
(a) Bipolar depression.
(b) Post-natal depression.
(c) Menopausal depression.

7 Cognitive theories of depression led to:
(a) CDT.
(b) CBT.
(c) ICT.

8 Which of the following is correct?
(a) All depression follows an activating event.
(b) Cognition is the root cause of all depression.
(c) Beck's theory does not explain all aspects of depression.

Answers
1C 2B 3A 4C
5C 6B 7B 8C

Possible extended writing questions:
- Discuss Beck's negative triad **and/or** Ellis' ABC model of depression. *[AS = 12, AL = 16]*
- Outline and evaluate the cognitive approach to explaining depression. *[AS = 12, AL = 16]*

A01 **A03**

Book-link

Y1/AS Student Book
Pages 150–151

Y1/AS Revision Guide
Pages 102–103

Spec Spotlight

The cognitive
approach to treating
depression: cognitive
behavior therapy
including challenging
irrational thoughts.

CBT (Beck)

Patient and therapist identify irrational thoughts.

Challenging negative thoughts – thoughts about the self, the world and the future.

'Patient as scientist' – test reality of beliefs through homework.

REBT (Ellis)

Extends ABC model, D for dispute beliefs, E for effect.

Challenging irrational beliefs – therapist uses empirical and logical arguments.

Behavioural activation to decrease avoidance and isolation.

$\oplus$ CBT as effective as antidepressants – together is best (March *et al.*).

$\ominus$ CBT may not work – in severe cases patient may lack motivation.

$\ominus$ Success may be due to patient–therapist relationship and not therapy itself.

$\ominus$ Some patients may want to explore their past – focus is on present only.

$\ominus$ Therapies overemphasise cognition and ignore patient's social circumstances.

Topic 4: PSYCHOPATHOLOGY

1 *Not* part of CBT:
(a) Identify irrational beliefs.
(b) Patient takes passive role.
(c) Patient completes homework.

2 A core concept of CBT:
(a) Patient as psychologist.
(b) Patient as scientist.
(c) Patient as therapist.

3 *Not* a feature of REBT:
(a) D for dispute.
(b) E for effect.
(c) F for finish.

4 *Not* a form of argument in REBT:
(a) Irrational.
(b) Logical.
(c) Empirical.

5 A method to decrease avoidance and isolation:
(a) Behavioural intention.
(b) Behavioural activation.
(c) Behavioural association.

6 Which is true of the March *et al.* study?
(a) CBT more effective than drugs.
(b) Drugs more effective than CBT.
(c) Drugs and CBT most effective.

7 Which of the following is true?
(a) CBT works best in severe cases.
(b) CBT underemphasises cognition.
(c) Success of CBT may depend on patient–therapist relationship.

8 In cognitive therapies, focus tends to be on the:
(a) Present.
(b) Past.
(c) Future.

Answers
1B 2B 3C 4A
5B 6C 7C 8A

Topic 4: PSYCHOPATHOLOGY

Possible extended writing questions:

- Discuss cognitive behaviour therapy as a way of treating depression. *[AS = 12, AL = 16]*
- Outline and evaluate the cognitive approach to treating depression. *[AS = 12, AL = 16]*

AO1 The biological approach to explaining OCD **AO3**

Topic 4: PSYCHOPATHOLOGY

Genetic explanation

Candidate genes for serotonin (5HT1-D) and dopamine.

Polygenic – evidence of up to 230 different genes (Taylor).

Different types of OCD may have different genes, and genes differ from person to person (aetiologically heterogenous).

(+) Support for genes – 68% concordance MZs, 31% DZs (Nestadt et al.).

(−) Too many candidate genes identified to have predictive value.

(−) Environmental risk from trauma – diathesis-stress (Cromer et al.).

Neural explanation

Low levels of serotonin lower mood.

Decision-making systems in frontal lobes impaired.

Left parahippocampal gyrus (unpleasant emotions) functions abnormally.

(+) Research support – antidepressants reduce OCD by increasing serotonin.

(−) Serotonin link to OCD – may be because patients are depressed (co-morbid).

(−) Diathesis-stress model – may be a better fit than neural alone.

Spec Spotlight

The biological approach to explaining OCD: genetic and neural explanations.

The biological approach to explaining OCD – multiple choice questions

1 *Not* implicated in the cause of OCD:
(a) Serotonin.
(b) Oxytocin.
(c) Dopamine.

2 Number of genes Taylor identified:
(a) 130.
(b) 230.
(c) 330.

3 Refers to different genes for OCD in different people:
(a) Aetiologically heterogenous.
(b) Biologically heterozygous.
(c) Theoretically heterozygous.

4 Frontal lobes responsible for:
(a) Perception.
(b) Conscious awareness.
(c) Decision making.

5 Area of parahippocampal gyrus that functions abnormally in OCD:
(a) Left.
(b) Middle.
(c) Right.

6 MZ concordance in Nestadt *et al.* study:
(a) 68%
(b) 50%
(c) 31%

7 The Cromer *et al.* study best supports:
(a) Biological factors in OCD.
(b) Environmental factors in OCD.
(c) The diathesis-stress model.

8 OCD patients may also be depressed. This is called:
(a) Concordance.
(b) Co-dependency.
(c) Co-morbidity.

Topic 4: PSYCHOPATHOLOGY

Answers
1B 2B 3A 4C
5A 6A 7C 8C

Possible extended writing questions:

- Discuss the biological approach to explaining OCD. *[AS = 12, AL = 16]*
- Outline and evaluate genetic **and** neural explanations for OCD. *[AS = 12, AL = 16]*

Y1/AS Student Book
Pages 154–155

Y1/AS Revision Guide
Pages 106–107

Drug therapy

Increases levels of the neurotransmitter serotonin.

SSRIs prevent the reabsorption and breakdown of serotonin in the brain.

Typical daily dose of *fluoxetine* (an SSRI) is 20–60mg, depending on effectiveness.

Combining SSRIs with CBT often most effective treatment.

Tricyclics (older type of antidepressant), e.g. *clomipramine*, are sometimes used.

Newer SNRIs increase levels of noradrenaline as well as serotonin.

⊕ Supporting evidence – 17 studies showed SSRIs more effective than placebos (Soomro *et al.*).

⊕ Drugs are cost-effective and non-disruptive compared to alternative treatments.

⊖ Drugs have side-effects – which may affect whether treatment continues.

⊖ Evidence favouring drug treatment – may be biased by drug company funding.

⊖ OCD often follows trauma – so biological treatments may be ineffective.

Spec Spotlight

The biological approach to treating OCD: drug therapy.

Topic 4: PSYCHOPATHOLOGY

The biological approach to treating OCD – multiple choice questions

1 SSRIs:
(a) Reduce levels of serotonin.
(b) Increase levels of serotonin.
(c) Have no effect on serotonin levels.

2 A type of SSRI:
(a) Fluoxetine.
(b) Flutoxin.
(c) Fluxotine.

3 Typical daily dosage of SSRIs is:
(a) 10–50mg.
(b) 20–60mg.
(c) 30–70mg.

4 Older antidepressants include:
(a) Climopremine.
(b) Clamipromine.
(c) Clomipramine.

5 SNRIs increase serotonin and:
(a) Noradrenaline.
(b) Adrenaline.
(c) Dopamine.

6 Soomro et al. analysed:
(a) 17 studies.
(b) 27 studies.
(c) 37 studies.

7 Compared to other treatments, drugs are:
(a) An active treatment.
(b) Time-consuming.
(c) Cost-effective.

8 Biological treatments may be ineffective because:
(a) OCD often follows trauma.
(b) OCD may have a neural basis.
(c) OCD has a physical not psychological origin.

Answers
1B 2A 3B 4C
5A 6A 7C 8A

Topic 4: PSYCHOPATHOLOGY

Possible extended writing questions:
- Discuss drug therapy as a way of treating OCD. *[AS = 12, AL = 16]*
- Outline and evaluate the biological approach to treating OCD. *[AS = 12, AL = 16]*

Spec Spotlight

Origins of psychology:
Wundt, introspection
and the emergence
of Psychology
as a science.

Wundt and introspection

Established first psychology lab.

Introspection – consciousness broken into
thoughts, images, sensations.

Recorded in standardised, controlled
conditions.

(+) Wundt's methods were scientific –
controlled and standardised.

(+) Forerunner to later scientific approaches.

(−) Some aspects not scientific –
e.g. subjective data.

Emergence of psychology as a science

1900s – Behaviourists (Watson, Skinner)
rejected introspection, lab experiments.

1950s – Cognitive approach, mental processes
studied.

1990s – Biological approach, objective
techniques, e.g. EEG, fMRI.

(+) Learning approaches, cognitive and
biological approach all use scientific
method.

(−) Some approaches – e.g. humanistic,
psychodynamic, are less scientific.

(−) Scientific study of human thought and
experience may not be possible.

1 **He established the first psychology lab:**
(a) Wundt.
(b) Watson.
(c) Williams.

2 **Wundt's method:**
(a) Introversion.
(b) Interception.
(c) Introspection.

3 **The approach that rejected introspection:**
(a) Behaviourism.
(b) Psychodynamic.
(c) Cognitive.

4 **A leading behaviourist:**
(a) Wundt.
(b) Watson.
(c) Williams.

5 **A weakness of Wundt's method:**
(a) Couldn't be standardised.
(b) Couldn't be replicated.
(c) Produced subjective data.

6 **An approach that does *not* use the scientific method:**
(a) Cognitive.
(b) Humanistic.
(c) Biological.

7 ***Not* part of introspection:**
(a) Thoughts.
(b) Images.
(c) Movements.

8 **Behaviourism favoured which method?**
(a) Case studies.
(b) Experiments.
(c) Interviews.

Topic 5: APPROACHES

Answers
1A 2C 3A 4B
5C 6B 7C 8B

Possible extended writing questions:

- Outline and discuss Wundt's contribution to psychology. *[AS = 6, AL = 8]*
- Discuss the emergence of psychology as a science. *[AS = 5, AL = 8]*

AO1

AO3

Book-link

Y1/AStudent Book
Pages 106–107

Y2/AL Student Book
Pages 10–11

Y1/AS Revision Guide
Pages 72–73

Y2/AL Revision Guide
Pages 12–13

Spec Spotlight

Learning approaches: The behaviourist approach including classical conditioning and Pavlov's research, operant conditioning, types of reinforcement and Skinner's research

---

Only concerned with observable behaviour that can be measured.

Controlled lab studies to remove bias and maintain objectivity.

Animals can be used because processes that govern learning are the same in all species.

Classical conditioning – learning through association, **Pavlov** (dog salivation: UCS, UCR, NS, CS, CR).

Operant conditioning – learning through consequences, **Skinner** (pigeons, rats, behaviour shaped by consequences).

Types of reinforcement – positive and negative, also positive and negative punishment.

$\oplus$ Gave psychology scientific credibility – objective measurement of behaviour.

$\oplus$ Real-life application – token economy used in prisons and psychiatry.

$\ominus$ Mechanistic view – humans and animals are passive responders.

$\ominus$ Environmental determinism – ignores conscious decision making.

$\ominus$ Animal research raises ethical issues and findings may lack validity.

Topic 5: APPROACHES

1 Behaviourists are *not* interested in studying phenomena that are:
(a) Measurable.
(b) Subjective.
(c) Observable.

2 Classical conditioning:
(a) Learning by association.
(b) Learning by consequence.
(c) Learning by reinforcement.

3 Pavlov investigated salivation in:
(a) Dogs.
(b) Cats.
(c) Pigeons.

4 *Not* a type of reinforcement:
(a) Positive.
(b) Negative.
(c) Punishment.

5 Behaviourists are most likely to use:
(a) Case studies.
(b) Lab experiments.
(c) Structured interviews.

6 Form of determinism associated with behaviourism:
(a) Psychic.
(b) Biological.
(c) Environmental.

7 A behavioural technique used in prisons and psychiatric wards:
(a) Anxiety hierarchy.
(b) Token economy.
(c) Introspection.

8 A strength of animal studies:
(a) Findings are valid.
(b) High degree of control.
(c) Ethical treatment.

Answers
1B 2A 3A 4C
5B 6C 7B 8B

Possible extended writing questions:

- Discuss the contribution of Pavlov **and/or** Skinner in psychology. *[AS = 12, AL = 16]*
- Outline and evaluate the behaviourist approach. *[AS = 12, AL = 16]*

AO1   AO3

Topic 5: APPROACHES

Book-link

Y1/AS Student Book
Pages 108–109

Y2/AL Student Book
Pages 12–13

Y1/AS Revision Guide
Pages 74–75

Y2/AL Revision Guide
Pages 14–15

Spec Spotlight

Learning approaches: social learning theory including imitation, identification, modelling, vicarious reinforcement, the role of mediational processes and Bandura's research.

Bandura research – learning indirectly, in a social context through observation and imitation.

Vicarious reinforcement – behaviour that is rewarded is more likely to be imitated.

Mediational processes – attention, retention, motor reproduction, motivation.

Identification – children imitate role models with whom they identify.

Imitation – Bandura's Bobo doll, aggression learned through imitating role models.

Modelling aggression – more likely if behaviour is vicariously rewarded.

(+) Importance of cognitive factors – emphasised by SLT, ignored by behaviourism.

(−) Controlled lab studies, creates demand characteristics – e.g. Bandura studies.

(−) Underestimates biological factors – e.g. testosterone in aggression.

(+) Can account for cultural differences in behaviour, e.g. gender role learning.

(+) Less determinist than the behaviourist approach – some choice in behaviour.

1 Indirect reward:
(a) Negative reinforcement.
(b) Vicarious reinforcement.
(c) Positive reinforcement.

2 *Not* a mediational process:
(a) Meditation.
(b) Motor reproduction.
(c) Motivation.

3 Children will imitate role models with whom they:
(a) Identify.
(b) Improvise.
(c) Initiate.

4 Bobo doll researcher:
(a) Bainbridge.
(b) Bannister.
(c) Bandura.

5 Imitating behaviour that has been seen to be rewarded:
(a) Mastering.
(b) Modelling.
(c) Monitoring.

6 SLT emphasises the role of:
(a) Psychic factors in learning.
(b) Cognitive factors in learning.
(c) Biological factors in learning.

7 A problem in Bandura's studies:
(a) Demand characteristics.
(b) Low control.
(c) Subjective data.

8 Compared to behaviourism, SLT is:
(a) More determinist.
(b) Less determinist.
(c) Just as determinist.

Answers
1B 2A 3A 4C
5B 6B 7A 8B

Possible extended writing questions:

- Outline and evaluate the social learning approach. Refer to **at least one** other approach in your answer. *[AS = 12, AL = 16]*
- Discuss the contribution of Bandura's research in psychology. *[AS = 12, AL = 16]*

AO1

AO3

Book-link

Y1/AS Student Book Pages 110–111

Y2/AL Student Book Pages 14–15

Y1/AS Revision Guide Pages 76–77

Y2/AL Revision Guide Pages 16–17

Spec Spotlight

The cognitive approach: the study of internal mental processes, the role of schema, the use of theoretical and computer models to explain and make inferences about mental processes. The emergence of cognitive neuroscience.

Scientific study of mental processes, e.g. perception and memory.

Internal mental processes – study 'private' mental processes by making assumptions (inferences).

Theoretical models – information flows through input, storage and retrieval stages.

Computer models – program computers to model human thinking (artificial intelligence).

Schemas – a mental framework to interpret incoming information, become more complex with experience.

Cognitive neuroscience – scientific study of how brain structures affect mental processes, e.g. linking prefrontal cortex to episodic and semantic memories.

⊕ Scientific, objective approach to studying the mind.

⊖ Machine reductionism – an oversimplification, e.g. no emotion.

⊖ Research lacks external validity – studies use artificial stimuli.

⊕ Real-life application to everyday life, e.g. robots.

⊕ Less determinist than other approaches – soft determinism.

Topic 5: APPROACHES

1 Making assumptions to study mental processes:
(a) Interference.
(b) Inference.
(c) Influence.

2 Cognitive neuroscience is:
(a) The study of how brain structures influence mental processes.
(b) The study of brain structures.
(c) The study of mental processes.

3 The approach that rejected introspection:
(a) Behaviourism.
(b) Psychodynamic.
(c) Cognitive.

4 A mental framework to interpret incoming information:
(a) Sensory memory.
(b) Cognitive process.
(c) Schema.

5 In a theoretical model, information flows through input, storage and:
(a) Retention.
(b) Retrieval.
(c) Recall.

6 Oversimplifying human cognitive processing:
(a) Mechanical reductionism.
(b) Machine reductionism.
(c) Mechanistic reductionism.

7 Type of determinism associated with the cognitive approach:
(a) Soft.
(b) Hard.
(c) Medium.

8 Research in the cognitive approach is often accused of:
(a) Lacking internal validity.
(b) Lacking external validity.
(c) Lacking temporal validity.

Answers
1B 2A 3A 4C
5B 6B 7A 8B

Possible extended writing questions:

- Outline and evaluate the cognitive approach. *[AS = 12, AL = 16]*
- Outline the cognitive approach. Discuss **at least two** differences between the cognitive approach and the behaviourist approach. *[AS = 12, AL = 16]*

Y1/AS Student Book
Pages 112–113

Y2/AL Student Book
Pages 16–17

Y1/AS Revision Guide
Pages 78–79

Y2/AL Revision Guide
Pages 18–19

Spec Spotlight

The biological approach: the influence of genes, biological structures and neurochemistry on behaviour. Genotype and phenotype, genetic basis of behaviour, evolution and behaviour.

Everything psychological is at first biological.

Genes and neurochemistry e.g. 5HT1-D beta gene and neurotransmiitter serotonin implicated in OCD.

The mind and body are one and the same.

Twin studies are used to investigate the genetic basis of behaviour.

Genotype – a person's genetic make-up.
Phenotype – the expression of the genotype.

Theory of evolution – behaviour that enhances survival and reproduction is naturally selected.

⊕ Highly scientific methods – e.g. fMRIs and drug trials.

⊕ Real-life application – the development of psychoactive drugs for mental illness.

⊖ Causal conclusions about neurotransmitters are difficult to establish.

⊖ Biological determinism – at odds with the legal system.

⊖ Nature and nurture are difficult to separate – e.g. in twin studies also have similar environments (confounding variable).

Topic 5: APPROACHES

1 *Not* a feature of the biological approach:
(a) Genetic influence.
(b) Neurochemical influence.
(c) Social influence.

2 *Not* a biological term:
(a) Genotype.
(b) Phenotype.
(c) Stereotype.

3 Charles Darwin's:
(a) Theory of evolution.
(b) Theory of revolution.
(c) Theory of elocution.

4 In the biological approach:
(a) The mind and body are separate.
(b) The mind and the body are the same.
(c) The mind has control over the body.

5 Twin studies are used to investigate:
(a) The neurochemical basis of behaviour.
(b) The genetic basis of behaviour.
(c) The cognitive basis of behaviour.

6 Biological determinism is at odds with:
(a) The legal system.
(b) The family system.
(c) The benefits system.

7 Chemical in the brain:
(a) Neuroconnectors.
(b) Neurotransmitters.
(c) Neurosynapses.

8 *Not* true of the biological approach:
(a) Highly precise methods.
(b) Led to development of psychoactive drugs.
(c) Causal conclusions are straightforward to establish.

Answers
1C 2C 3A 4B
5B 6A 7B 8C

Possible extended writing questions:

- Discuss the biological approach in psychology. *[AS = 12, AL = 16]*
- Outline the biological approach. Compare the biological approach with **one other** approach in psychology. *[AS = 12, AL = 16]*

Book-link

Y1/AS Student Book Pages 118–119

Y2/AL Student Book Pages 18–19

Y1/AS Revision Guide Pages 84–85

Y2/AL Revision Guide Pages 20–21

Spec Spotlight

The psychodynamic approach: the role of the unconscious, the structure of personality, that is Id, Ego and Superego, defence mechanisms including repression, denial and displacement, psychosexual stages.

A01

Unconscious mind – important influence on behaviour.

Tripartite **structure of personality** – **id**, **ego**, **superego** interact.

Five **psychosexual stages** determine adult personality, conflict leads to 'fixation'.

The sequence of stages is fixed – oral, anal, phallic, latency, genital.

Oedipus complex occurs at the phallic stage in boys, penis envy in girls.

Defence mechanisms control the id and reduce ego anxiety – **repression**, **denial**, **displacement**.

A03

(+) Explanatory power – huge influence on Western contemporary thought.

(−) Relied on small number of case studies – unscientific, subjective method.

(−) Untestable concepts – unfalsifiable pseudoscience.

(+) Real-life application – psychoanalysis to access the unconscious (though only suitable for mild neuroses, not psychotic disorders).

(−) Psychic determinism – childhood source of all behaviour, extreme position.

Topic 5: APPROACHES

91

The psychodynamic approach – *multiple choice questions*

1 *Not* one of Freud's levels of consciousness:
(a) Preconscious.
(b) Subconscious.
(c) Unconscious.

2 'Selfish instinctive drives' best Describes:
(a) Id.
(b) Ego.
(c) Superego.

3 In psychodynamic theory, conflict leads to:
(a) Stagnation.
(b) Fixation.
(c) Inertia.

4 Oral, anal, _____ , latency, genital:
(a) Plastic.
(b) Pyrrhic.
(c) Phallic.

5 'Forcing distressing memories into the unconscious mind':
(a) Repression.
(b) Denial.
(c) Displacement.

6 The name of Freudian therapy:
(a) Cognitive behaviour therapy.
(b) Client-centred therapy.
(c) Psychoanalysis.

7 Form of determinism most associated with Freud:
(a) Psychic.
(b) Biological.
(c) Environmental.

8 In psychodynamic therapy, focus tends to be on the:
(a) Present.
(b) Past.
(c) Future.

Topic 5: APPROACHES

Answers
1B 2A 3B 4C
5A 6C 7A 8B

Possible extended writing questions:
- Discuss the psychodynamic approach. Refer to **at least one** topic you have studied in your answer. *[AL = 16]*
- Outline and evaluate the psychodynamic approach. *[AL = 16]*

Spec Spotlight

Humanistic psychology: free will, self-actualisation and Maslow's hierarchy of needs, focus on the self, congruence, the role of conditions of worth. The influence of counselling Psychology.

A01

Free will and the study of the subjective experience of unique individuals.

Maslow's hierarchy of needs – work towards self-actualisation.

The self refers to 'I' and 'me', what I am and what I can do.

Congruence – client-centred therapy (CCT) aims for harmony between self-concept and ideal self.

Conditions of worth – imposed by parents, may prevent personal growth.

Counselling (CCT, Rogers) – genuine, empathic, unconditional positive regard.

A03

⊕ Anti-reductionist – holistic approach has more validity.

⊖ Limited application – lacks a sound evidence base.

⊕ Portrays a positive image of the human condition.

⊖ Untestable concepts – abstract, vague ideas that are difficult to test.

⊖ Western cultural bias – more associated with individualism.

Topic 5: APPROACHES

The humanistic approach – *multiple choice questions*

1 The aim of CCT is to establish:
- (a) Congruence.
- (b) Incongruence.
- (c) Imbalance.

2 Imposed by parents, they can restrict personal growth:
- (a) Conditions of worth.
- (b) Consequences of self.
- (c) Comparisons with others.

3 *Not* part of CCT:
- (a) Genuineness.
- (b) Empathy.
- (c) Conditional positive regard.

4 Proposed the hierarchy of needs:
- (a) Mason.
- (b) Maslow.
- (c) Maynard.

5 The uppermost level of the hierarchy:
- (a) Self-application.
- (b) Self-transformation.
- (c) Self-actualisation.

6 The humanistic approach is:
- (a) Anti-reductionist.
- (b) Pro-determinist.
- (c) Anti-holistic.

7 The cultural bias in the humanistic approach favours:
- (a) Individualism.
- (b) Collectivism.
- (c) Socialism.

8 Introduced client-centred therapy:
- (a) Richards.
- (b) Robson.
- (c) Rogers.

Answers
1A 2A 3C 4B
5C 6A 7A 8C

Topic 5: APPROACHES

Possible extended writing questions:

- Discuss **two or more** similarities between the humanistic approach and the psychodynamic approach. *[AL = 16]*
- Outline and evaluate the humanistic approach. *[AL = 16]*

Y1/AS Student Book
Pages 122–123

Y2/AL Student Book
Pages 22–23

Y1/AS Revision Guide
Pages 88–89

Y2/AL Revision Guide
Pages 24–25

Spec Spotlight

Comparison of
approaches.

Approach	Behaviourist	Social Learning	Cognitive	Biological	Psychodynamic	Humanistic
Views on development	Continuous processes		Stage theories, schema	Innate, maturational changes	St... co... ...ture an... ...tur...	Development of self
Nature versus nurture	Blank slate	Blank slate + observation/ imitation	Innate information processing + experience	Genes inherited	B... ...es + ...ut	Unconditional positive regard from others
Reductionism	Stimulus-response units	Interaction of cognitive + environment	Machine reductionism	Level of gene or neuron	H... ...ion	Anti-reductionist
Determinism	Environmental determinism	Reciprocal determinism	Soft determinism	Genetic determinism	P... hic...	Self-determinism (free will)
Abnormal behaviour	Faulty learning	Inappropriate modelling	Faulty thinking	Chemical imbalance		Conditions of worth

95

A level only

Comparison of approaches – *multiple choice questions*

1 **Which sees the self as central to development?**
(a) Humanistic.
(b) Cognitive.
(c) Behaviourist.

2 **Which does *not* see humans as blank slates at birth?**
(a) Social learning theory.
(b) Biological.
(c) Behaviourist.

3 **Form of reductionism associated with the cognitive approach:**
(a) Electronic.
(b) Digital.
(c) Machine.

4 **Reciprocal determinism:**
(a) Cognitive.
(b) Social learning theory.
(c) Psychodynamic.

5 **Anti-reductionist:**
(a) Humanistic.
(b) Behaviourist.
(c) Biological.

6 **Abnormal behaviour as a result of unconscious conflicts:**
(a) Cognitive.
(b) Humanistic.
(c) Psychodynamic.

7 ***Not* associated with stage theories of development:**
(a) Biological.
(b) Behaviourist.
(c) Cognitive.

8 **Soft determinism:**
(a) Cognitive.
(b) Behaviourist.
(c) Biological.

Answers
1A 2B 3C 4B
5A 6C 7B 8A

Possible extended writing questions:

- Outline and compare any **two** approaches in psychology. *[AL = 16]*
- Discuss **two** similarities between the psychodynamic approach and the humanistic approach. *[AL = 16]*

Book-link

Y1/AS Student Book
Pages 114–115

Y2/A Student Book
Pages 34–35

Y1/AS Revision Guide
Pages 80–81

Y2/A Revision Guide
Pages 26–27

Spec Spotlight

The divisions
of the nervous system:
central and peripheral
(somatic and autonomic).
The function of the
endocrine system: glands
and hormones.
The fight or flight
response and the role
of adrenaline.

The nervous system AO1

Key features – network of specialised cells,
primary communication system.

Collects, processes, responds to information
in environment, co-ordinates organs/cells.

Central nervous system (CNS)

Brain – conscious awareness, includes
cerebral cortex (higher mental functions).

Spinal cord – extension of brain, reflexes.

Peripheral nervous system (PNS)

Autonomic nervous system (ANS) – governs
vital bodily functions (e.g. stress response).

Somatic nervous system (SNS) – controls
muscles and information from senses.

The endocrine system AO1

Key features – controls functions via hormones
(slower than NS but widespread).

Glands – organs producing hormones,
e.g. pituitary ('master gland'), controls others.

Hormones – in bloodstream, affect organs
with receptors, e.g. thyroxine → heart.

Fight or flight response

(1) Hypothalamus detects stressor.

(2) Hypothalamus triggers sympathetic ANS,
initiates state of physiological arousal.

(3) **Adrenaline** from adrenal medulla, triggers arousal in target organs (e.g. heart).

(4) Threat passes, parasympathetic ANS
returns body to 'rest and digest'.

1 The two major systems of the nervous system are:
(a) Central and peripheral.
(b) Autonomic and somatic.
(c) Brain and spinal cord.

2 The cerebral cortex is part of the:
(a) Peripheral nervous system.
(b) Spinal cord.
(c) Brain.

3 The autonomic nervous system is part of the:
(a) Central nervous system.
(b) Peripheral nervous system.
(c) Somatic nervous system.

4 The somatic nervous system:
(a) Controls higher mental functions.
(b) Governs the stress response.
(c) Controls movements of muscles.

5 The master gland of the endocrine system is the:
(a) Pituitary.
(b) Adrenal medulla.
(c) Pancreas.

6 Hormones:
(a) Have narrower effects than the NS.
(b) Work more slowly than the NS.
(c) Travel along nerves.

7 The main hormone involved in the fight or flight response is:
(a) Adrenaline.
(b) Insulin.
(c) Oestrogen.

8 The rest and digest response is governed by the:
(a) Spinal cord.
(b) Pituitary gland.
(c) Parasympathetic nervous system.

Topic 6: BIOPSYCHOLOGY

Answers
1A 2C 3B 4C
5A 6B 7A 8C

Possible extended writing questions:
- Outline the divisions of the nervous system. [AS and AL = 4]
- Briefly explain the function of the endocrine system. [AS and AL = 4]
- Describe the fight or flight response, including the role of adrenaline. [AS and AL = 6]

Book-link

Spec Spotlight

The structure and function of sensory, relay and motor neurons. The process of synaptic transmission, including reference to neurotransmitters, excitation and inhibition.

A01 Neurons

Motor – connect CNS to effectors (muscles and glands), short dendrites/long axons.

Sensory – carry messages from PNS to CNS, long dendrites/short axons.

Relay – connect sensory to motor or other relay, short dendrites/short axons.

Structure of neuron

Cell body – nucleus, dendrites protrude.

Axon – carries impulse away from cell body, covered in myelin sheath, nodes of Ranvier.

Terminal buttons – meet next neuron/synapse.

Electric transmission

Activated neuron – positive charge creates action potential (impulse).

Synaptic transmission A01

Chemical transmission – signals between neurons across synapse (gap) are chemical.

Impulse reaches end of neuron, triggers vesicles (sacs) to release neurotransmitter.

Neurotransmitter crosses synapse, binds with receptors on next neuron.

Neurotransmitters – each has molecular structure fitting a receptor ('key in lock').

Excitation – some neurotransmitters make next neuron more likely to fire (adrenaline).

Inhibition – some neurotransmitters make next neuron less likely to fire (serotonin).

Summation – many excitatory and inhibitory influences on neuron, must reach threshold.

1 Sensory neurons:
(a) Have long axons.
(b) Connect other neurons.
(c) Carry messages from PNS to CNS.

2 The structure carrying impulses away from the cell body is the:
(a) Nucleus.
(b) Axon.
(c) Dendrites.

3 The structure communicating across the synapse is the:
(a) Cell body.
(b) Nodes of Ranvier.
(c) Terminal button.

4 An electrical impulse travelling down an axon is called the:
(a) Action potential.
(b) Positive charge.
(c) Relay.

5 At the end of a neuron, an impulse triggers _____ to release _____.
(a) Axons, vesicles.
(b) Vesicles, neurotransmitter.
(c) Dendrites, synapses.

6 Chemical transmission takes place:
(a) Across neurons.
(b) Across a synapse.
(c) Along an axon.

7 The effect of serotonin is:
(a) Inhibitory.
(b) Excitatory.
(c) Neutral.

8 Excitatory and inhibitory influences are summed and must:
(a) Cancel each other out.
(b) Reach a threshold.
(c) Be exactly the same.

Answers
1C 2B 3C 4A
5B 6B 7A 8B

Possible extended writing questions:

- Describe the structure and function of sensory, relay and motor neurons. *[AS and AL = 6]*
- Outline the process of synaptic transmission. *[AS and AL = 6]*

Book-link

Y2/A Student Book
Page 38–39
Y2/A Revision Guide
Pages 30–31

Spec Spotlight

Localisation of function in the brain: motor, somatosensory, visual, auditory and language centres; Broca's and Wernicke's areas.

Holism – once thought all brain involved in all functions, now clear specific areas control specific functions.

Two brain hemispheres – left of body controlled by right and vice versa.

Cerebral cortex – outer layer (3mm) of brain, advanced functions in humans.

Lobes – frontal (**motor**), parietal (**somatosensory**), temporal (**auditory**), occipital (**visual**).

Language centres

Broca's area – left frontal lobe, speech production, damage Broca's aphasia.

Wernicke's area – left temporal lobe, language comprehension.

(+) Brain scan evidence – Broca's area active in listening, Wernicke's in reading (Peterson *et al.*).

(+) Neurological evidence – cingulotomy improved symptoms in OCD patients (Dougherty *et al.*).

(+) Case studies – e.g. Phineas Gage, frontal lobe damage led to personality change.

(−) Contradictory research – cognitive functions distributed holistically throughout brain (Lashley).

(−) Neural plasticity after trauma – brain reorganises, law of equipotentiality.

Topic 6: BIOPSYCHOLOGY

A level only

Localisation of function in the brain – multiple choice questions

1 The alternative to localisation is:
(a) All-brain theory.
(b) Contra-localisation.
(c) Holism.

2 There are two brain hemispheres, which are:
(a) Sinister and dexter.
(b) Left and right.
(c) Higher and lower.

3 The cerebral cortex in humans controls:
(a) All physiological functions.
(b) Advanced functions like thinking.
(c) Basic functions like heart rate.

4 Wernicke's area:
(a) Controls language understanding.
(b) Is in the left frontal lobe.
(c) Is in the right temporal lobe.

5 In brain scan studies, the area of the brain most active when we are listening is:
(a) The right hemisphere.
(b) Broca's area.
(c) Wernicke's area.

6 OCD patients' symptoms improve when treated using a:
(a) Lobotomy.
(b) Brain scan.
(c) Cingulotomy.

7 Phineas Gage experienced damage to his:
(a) Occipital lobe.
(b) Frontal lobe.
(c) Temporal lobe.

8 The brain's ability to reorganise after damage is called:
(a) Neural plasticity.
(b) Neural elasticity.
(c) Neural electricity.

Topic 6: BIOPSYCHOLOGY

Answers
1C 2B 3B 4A
5B 6C 7B 8A

Possible extended writing questions:

- Discuss localisation of function in the brain. Refer in your answer to **at least two** brain areas you have studied. *[AL = 16]*
- Outline and evaluate research into localisation of function in the brain. *[AL = 16]*

A01   # Plasticity and functional recovery of the brain   **A03**

Brain plasticity

Synaptic connections form and are pruned throughout life.

Learning 'the knowledge' changes a taxi driver's hippocampus (Maguire *et al.*).

Changes to hippocampus in medical students around exams (Draganski *et al.*).

Functional recovery

Healthy brain areas take over lost functions after trauma.

Brain reorganises and rewires – new synaptic connections, secondary pathways 'unmasked'.

Structural changes – axonal sprouting, similar areas opposite side of brain used.

(+) Real-life application – help cognitive functioning after stroke (neuro-rehabilitation).

(−) Negative consequences – plasticity not always beneficial (phantom limb pain).

(−) Complex link with age – plasticity continues through lifespan, e.g. golf training (Bezzola *et al.*).

(+) Animal studies – kitten, one part of visual cortex took over processing (Hubel and Wiesel).

(−) Cognitive reserve – more education gives better chance of full recovery.

Topic 6: BIOPSYCHOLOGY

Spec Spotlight

Plasticity and functional recovery of the brain after trauma.

A level only

Plasticity and functional recovery of the brain – *multiple choice questions*

1 Synapses in the brain are pruned:
(a) Only in childhood.
(b) Throughout the lifespan.
(c) Only in the womb.

2 Maguire *et al*. studied:
(a) Taxi drivers.
(b) Medical students.
(c) The hypothalamus.

3 After trauma, the brain:
(a) Forms new synaptic connections.
(b) Activates dormant neural circuits.
(c) Both of the above.

4 One form of brain restructuring is:
(a) Myelin turniping.
(b) Axonal sprouting.
(c) Dendritic carroting.

5 Neuro-rehabilitation:
(a) Improves cognitive functioning.
(b) Has no effect on brain recovery.
(c) Involves removing the hippocampus.

6 Neural plasticity:
(a) Is always beneficial.
(b) Sometimes has negative consequences.
(c) Always has negative consequences.

7 Plasticity appears to:
(a) Increase with age.
(b) Extend through the lifespan.
(c) Be limited to childhood.

8 The chances of recovery are better in people with:
(a) Less cognitive reserve.
(b) Less education.
(c) More education.

Topic 6: BIOPSYCHOLOGY

Answers
1B 2A 3C 4B
5A 6B 7B 8C

Possible extended writing questions:

- Describe and evaluate research into plasticity **and/or** functional recovery of the brain after trauma. *[AL = 16]*
- Discuss plasticity **and** functional recovery of the brain after trauma. *[AL = 16]*

AO1   AO3

Book-link

Y2/A Student Book
Page 42–43

Y2/A Revision Guide
Pages 34–35

Hemispheric lateralisation

E.g. language controlled by left hemisphere (LH).

Split-brain research

Commissurotomy to control epilepsy, cut corpus callosum.

Sperry's procedure – one image/word to RVF, another to LVF, for very brief exposure.

Object shown to RVF (LH, language) patient describes object, shown to LVF (RH) 'nothing there'.

Object shown to LVF – cannot name (RH) but pick item with left hand.

Two halves of different faces – LH dominates description, RH dominates selection of matching picture.

⊕ Support – LH analyser, RH synthesiser, may be oversimplistic.

⊕ Good methodology – Sperry used controlled standardised procedure.

⊕ Started debate on brain – duality in brain or highly integrated hemispheres?

⊖ Generalisation – lacking because split-brain patients had epilepsy (i.e. unusual sample).

⊖ Overstated case – simplistic distinction between hemispheres, they may be more flexible.

Topic 6: BIOPSYCHOLOGY

Spec Spotlight

Hemispheric lateralisation: split-brain research.

A level only

Split-brain research into hemispheric lateralisation – *multiple choice questions*

1 The operation used on patients in a split-brain study is a:
(a) Hemispherectomy.
(b) Lobotomy.
(c) Commissurotomy.

2 In Sperry's procedure, one word or image is presented:
(a) To one hemisphere at a time.
(b) To both hemispheres at once.
(c) For at least one minute.

3 The patient *cannot* describe an object presented to the:
(a) Left visual field.
(b) Right visual field.
(c) Left hemisphere.

4 When an object is shown to the LVF, the patient can:
(a) Describe it.
(b) Name it.
(c) Pick it up with their left hand.

5 Research shows the left hemisphere is:
(a) A 'synthesiser'.
(b) An 'analyser'.
(c) A 'compromiser'.

6 Sperry's procedure was:
(a) Uncontrolled.
(b) Unreliable.
(c) Standardised.

7 Sperry's participants were:
(a) Representative of most people.
(b) Many and varied.
(c) Very unusual with unique brains.

8 In reality, the left and right hemispheres:
(a) Do not communicate.
(b) Are highly flexible.
(c) Differ in every way.

Topic 6: BIOPSYCHOLOGY

Answers
1C 2A 3A 4C
5B 6C 7C 8B

Possible extended writing questions:

- Discuss research into hemispheric lateralisation. *[AL = 16]*
- Outline and evaluate split-brain research. *[AL = 16]*

Book-link

Y2/A Student Book
Page 44–45
Y2/A Revision Guide
Pages 36–37

Topic 6: BIOPSYCHOLOGY

Spec Spotlight

Ways of studying the brain: scanning techniques, including functional magnetic resonance imaging (fMRI); electro-encephalograms (EEGs) and event-related potentials (ERPs); post-mortem examinations

fMRI

Detects increased oxygenation and blood flow in active brain areas, 3D.

(+) Non-invasive, no radiation. High spatial resolution.

(−) Expensive. Poor temporal resolution.

EEG

Electrodes measure overall electrical activity of millions of neurons.

(+) Diagnosing epilepsy. High temporal resolution.

(−) Signal comes from 1000s of neurons. Can't identify source.

ERPs

Statistical techniques enable extraneous brain activity to be filtered from EEGs.

(+) More specific than raw EEG data. High temporal resolution.

(−) No standardised procedure. Background noise.

Post-mortems

Analysis of brain after death, identify area of damage linked to cognitive deficit.

(+) Useful for understanding brain and for medical knowledge.

(−) Causation is an issue. Ethical issues over permission.

A level only

Ways of studying the brain – *multiple choice questions*

1 The 'f' in 'fMRI' stands for:
  (a) Functional.
  (b) Factual.
  (c) Formative.

2 EEGs measure the _____ activity of neurons.
  (a) Magnetic.
  (b) Electrical.
  (c) Overall.

3 ERPs are an enhanced form of the:
  (a) Post-mortem.
  (b) fMRI.
  (c) EEG.

4 A post-mortem:
  (a) Occurs before birth.
  (b) Is conducted after death.
  (c) Tells us how the brain works.

5 A strength of fMRI is that it:
  (a) Is invasive.
  (b) Does not use radiation.
  (c) Uses electrodes.

6 A limitation of EEG is:
  (a) It targets very specific areas.
  (b) It is the most expensive method.
  (c) The signal comes from many neurons.

7 A limitation of ERPs is:
  (a) They are dangerous.
  (b) They only provide general data.
  (c) Studies have no standardised procedure.

8 A strength of post-mortems is they are:
  (a) A good basis for understanding the brain.
  (b) Useful for diagnosing epilepsy.
  (c) Non-invasive.

Answers
1A 2B 3C 4B
5B 6C 7C 8A

Possible extended writing questions:

- Outline and evaluate **two or more** ways of studying the brain. *[AL = 16]*
- Discuss functional magnetic resonance imaging and **one other** way of studying the brain. *[AS = 12, AL = 16]*

| A01 | Biological rhythms: Circadian rhythms | A03 |

Topic 6: BIOPSYCHOLOGY

Rhythms governed by – endogenous pacemakers (EPs, internal clocks) and exogenous zeitgebers (EZs, external cues).

Circadian rhythm – approximately 24-hour cycle (e.g. sleep/wake cycle).

Sleep/wake – basic rhythm governed by SCN (EP), reset by daylight (EZ).

Siffre – cave/case studies (no light), free-running cycle regular but about 25 hours.

Aschoff and Wever – bunker studies, natural rhythm 25 hours entrained by EZs.

Folkhard *et al.* – hard to adjust to shorter day, stronger influence of EPs over EZs.

(+) Real-life application – link between shift work and ill-health, economic implications (Knutsson).

(+) Real-life application – pharmacokinetics, drugs more effective certain times day/night.

(−) Case studies – individuals (Siffre) and unrepresentative and small sample sizes, limits meaningful generalisations.

(−) Poor control – artificial light in studies affects rhythm, confounding variable.

(−) Individual differences – cycle lengths vary (13 to 65 hours, Czeisler *et al.*), 'larks' and 'owls' (Duffy *et al.*).

Spec Spotlight

Biological rhythms: circadian rhythms

Biological rhythms: Circadian rhythms – *multiple choice questions*

1 Endogenous pacemakers are:
(a) Circadian rhythms.
(b) External cues such as daylight.
(c) Internal biological clocks.

2 A circadian cycle is approximately:
(a) 1 day.
(b) 1 week.
(c) 1 month.

3 Michel Siffre's free-running sleep/wake cycle was:
(a) 23 hours.
(b) 25 hours.
(c) 29 hours.

4 Folkhard et al. suggested that the strongest influence on rhythms is:
(a) EZs.
(b) Daylight.
(c) EPs.

5 Pharmacokinetics shows that drugs:
(a) Can work very quickly.
(b) Are more effective at some points in the day–night cycle.
(c) Have nothing to do with rhythms.

6 Case studies of circadian rhythms:
(a) Produce unrepresentative findings.
(b) Are easily generalisable.
(c) Usually have many participants.

7 A confounding variable in some circadian rhythm research is:
(a) Access to artificial light.
(b) Different sizes of EPs.
(c) Good experimental control.

8 People's circadian cycles can vary from 13 hours to:
(a) 1 week.
(b) 25 hours.
(c) 65 hours.

Answers

1C 2A 3B 4C
5B 6A 7A 8C

Topic 6: BIOPSYCHOLOGY

Possible extended writing questions:

- Discuss research into biological rhythms. *[AL = 16]*
- Describe and evaluate research into circadian rhythms. *[AL = 16]*

AO1	Biological rhythms: Intradian and ultradian rhythms	AO3

Infradian rhythm

Menstrual cycle about 28 days, oestrogen/progesterone.	⊕ Started debate on brain – duality in brain or highly integrated hemispheres?
EZs synchronise cycles – pheromones, odour donors (Stern and McClintock).	⊖ Methodology – synchrony studies, small samples, confounding variables (e.g. stress).
SAD – seasonal depression, circannual (yearly), special type of infradian rhythm.	⊖ Animal studies of pheromones – e.g. sea urchins, less so in humans
Melatonin – longer secretion in winter because less light, low serotonin.	⊕ Started debate on brain – duality in brain or highly integrated hemispheres?

Ultradian rhythm

Sleep – 90-minute cycle of 5 stages, differing brain activity.	⊕ Supporting research – REM qualitatively distinct stage of ultradian sleep cycle (Dement and Kleitman).
Stages 1 & 2 light sleep alpha/beta waves, stages 3 & 4 deep sleep delta waves, REM (dreaming) brain active.	

Spec Spotlight

Biological rhythms: infradian and ultradian rhythms.

A level only

Biological rhythms: Infradian and ultradian rhythms – *multiple choice questions*

1 An example of an infradian rhythm is the:
(a) Sleep/wake cycle.
(b) Menstrual cycle.
(c) Stages of sleep.

2 **Stern and McClintock** investigated the effect of:
(a) Hormones.
(b) Pheromones.
(c) Cotton wool pads.

3 Seasonal affective disorder is:
(a) An ultradian rhythm.
(b) A circadian rhythm.
(c) A circannual rhythm.

4 Stages 3 and 4 of sleep are associated with:
(a) Alpha waves.
(b) Beta waves.
(c) Delta waves.

5 Research suggests that synchronised menstrual cycles have:
(a) No value.
(b) Evolutionary value.
(c) Financial value.

6 Animal studies show the importance of:
(a) Pheromones.
(b) Dreaming sleep.
(c) The menstrual cycle.

7 SAD has been treated using:
(a) Phototherapy.
(b) Photography.
(c) Photosynthesis.

8 Research shows that REM is:
(a) A distinct stage of sleep.
(b) A defunct rock band.
(c) Part of the menstrual cycle.

Topic 6: BIOPSYCHOLOGY

Answers
1B 2B 3C 4C
5B 6A 7A 8A

Possible extended writing questions:

- Outline and evaluate research into **two or more** biological rhythms. *[AS = 12, AL = 16]*
- Discuss research into infradian **and/or** ultradian rhythms. *[AS = 12, AL = 16]*

Endogenous pacemakers (EPs)

SCN (in hypothalamus) is primary EP.

Chipmunks and hamsters – transplanted SCNs, show importance (DeCoursey *et al.*, Ralph *et al.*).

SCN indicates day length to pineal gland which secretes melatonin when dark.

Exogenous zeitgebers (EZs)

'Time givers' – reset EPs by entrainment.

Light – entrains SCN to 24 hours, even via backs of knees (Campbell and Murphy).

Other EZs – babies entrained by 6 weeks, parents' social routines key influence.

⊖ Other body clocks – e.g. lungs, liver, independent of SCN, affect sleep-wake.

⊖ Use of animals – hard to generalise to humans, cognitive influences.

⊖ Overstated influence – blind man functioned OK (Miles), EZs only had small role.

⊖ Methodology – confounding variables, failure to replicate, overemphasis on light.

⊖ Interaction – EPs rarely free-run without EZs in real life, cave studies unrealistic.

Topic 6: BIOPSYCHOLOGY

Spec Spotlight

The effect of endogenous pacemakers and exogenous zeitgebers on the sleep/wake cycle.

Endogenous pacemakers and exogenous zeitgebers – *multiple choice questions*

1 The main endogenous pacemaker is:
(a) In the hippocampus.
(b) The suprachiasmatic nucleus.
(c) Daylight.

2 More melatonin is secreted:
(a) At night-time.
(b) During daylight.
(c) In the summer months.

3 Zeitgebers reset endogenous pacemakers by:
(a) Containment.
(b) Entrainment.
(c) Entertainment.

4 Campbell and Murphy used light to influence the SCN via the:
(a) Back of the knee.
(b) Crook of the elbow.
(c) Foot of the stairs.

5 There is/are:
(a) Just one body clock.
(b) One main body clock and many other less central ones.
(c) Several equally influential body clocks.

6 Research on a blind man showed that EZs:
(a) Are irrelevant to the sleep/wake cycle.
(b) Only play a small role.
(c) Have a large effect.

7 The EZ that has been studied much more than any other is:
(a) Social activities.
(b) Routine schedules.
(c) Light.

8 Which statement is true?
(a) EPs free-run often in real life.
(b) EZs are more important than EPs.
(c) EPs and EZs interact in real life.

Topic 6: BIOPSYCHOLOGY

Answers
1B 2A 3B 4A
5B 6C 7C 8C

Possible extended writing questions:

- Discuss the effect of endogenous pacemakers **and** exogenous zeitgebers on the sleep/wake cycle. *[AL = 16]*
- Describe and evaluate research into the effect of exogenous zeitgebers on the sleep/wake cycle. *[AL = 16]*

Y1/AS Student Book
Pages 166–169

Y1/AS Revision Guide
Page 108

Spec Spotlight

Aims: stating aims,
the difference between
aims and hypotheses.
Hypotheses: directional and
non-directional. Experimental
method. Variables: including
independent, dependent,
extraneous, confounding;
operationalisation of variables.
Demand characteristics
and investigator effects.
Randomisation and
standardisation.

Key concepts	Research issues	Research techniques
Aim – what researcher intends to investigate, general.	**Extraneous variables** – nuisance, do not systematically vary with IV.	**Randomisation** – nuisance, do not systematically vary with IV.
Hypothesis – **operationalised** (measurable), specific, **directional** and **non-directional**.	**Confounding variables** – vary systematically with IV, obscure effect of IV, must be controlled.	**Standardisation** – vary systematically with IV, obscure effect of IV, must be controlled.
Experimental method – researcher varies **independent variable** (IV) and measures effect on **dependent variable** (DV). Different levels of IV.	**Demand characteristics** – cues from researcher/ research situation, reveal aim.	Control groups – 'baseline' for comparison, establish causation.
	Investigator effects – effect of researcher's behaviour on DV.	Blinding – participant (single) plus researcher (double) don't know aims.

Topic 7: RESEARCH METHODS

(115)

1 An aim is a _____ statement.
  (a) General.
  (b) Precise.
  (c) Specific.

2 An operationalised variable is one that is:
  (a) Uncontrollable.
  (b) Predictable.
  (c) Measurable.

3 Two types of hypothesis are:
  (a) Directional and non-directional.
  (b) Left and right.
  (c) Up and down.

4 The variable manipulated by the researcher is:
  (a) Extraneous.
  (b) Dependent.
  (c) Independent.

5 A confounding variable:
  (a) Has random effects on the DV.
  (b) Varies systematically with the IV.
  (c) Is measured by the researcher.

6 A cue in a research situation that reveals the aim refers to:
  (a) Extraneous variable.
  (b) Investigator effect.
  (c) Demand characteristic.

7 A control group:
  (a) Provides a baseline for comparison.
  (b) Should be operationalised.
  (c) Should be non-directional.

8 Using the same procedure for all participants is:
  (a) Randomisation.
  (b) Standardisation.
  (c) Blinding.

Answers
1A 2C 3A 4C
5B 6C 7A 8B

Practice questions:

Two groups of participants read a list of ten words. One group then carried out an unrelated task before recalling the words. The other group recalled the words without carrying out the task.

1. Write a suitable directional hypothesis for this study. *[AS and AL = 2]*
2. State the operationalised IV and DV for this study. *[AS and AL = 2 + 2]*
3. Explain how randomisation and standardisation could have been used in this study. *[AS and AL = 2 + 2]*

Spec Spotlight

Experimental designs:
repeated measures,
independent groups,
matched pairs.

Topic 7: RESEARCH METHODS

Independent groups

| One group Condition A, another group Condition B, random allocation. | ⊕ | No order effects (tested once), no practice/fatigue. | ⊖ | Participant variables – different participants each group, EV/CV. |
| | ⊕ | Will not guess aim (tested once), natural behaviour. | ⊖ | More Ps – need twice as many as repeated measures. |

Repeated measures

| Each P does all conditions of IV, counterbalancing to avoid order effects | ⊕ | No participant variables (same people), controls EV/CV. | ⊖ | Order effects – similar task done twice, practice/fatigue, EV/CV. |
| | ⊕ | Fewer participants – half of independent groups. | ⊖ | Guess aims – easier when both conditions, change behaviour. |

Matched pairs

| Two separate groups but participants paired on participant variable(s). | ⊕ | No participant variables – reduced through matching. | ⊖ | Imperfect matching – takes time, not all relevant variables. |
| | ⊕ | No order effects (tested once), no practice fatigue. | ⊖ | More Ps – need twice as many as repeated measures. |

1 Matched pairs is a type of:
(a) Experimental control.
(b) Experimental method.
(c) Experimental design.

2 In an independent groups design:
(a) Matching can be imperfect.
(b) There are participant variables.
(c) The participant groups are related.

3 There are order effects in:
(a) Repeated measures.
(b) Independent groups.
(c) Matched pairs.

4 All participants carry out both conditions of the IV in:
(a) Matched pairs.
(b) Independent groups.
(c) Repeated measures.

5 A solution to order effects is:
(a) Counterbalancing.
(b) Countermeasuring.
(c) Countersigning.

6 It is easiest for participants to guess aims in:
(a) Independent groups.
(b) Repeated measures.
(c) Matched pairs.

7 In matched pairs, participants are matched on:
(a) Any relevant participant variable.
(b) Age and gender.
(c) Attractiveness.

8 Everything else being equal, which requires fewest participants?
(a) Independent participants.
(b) Repeated measures.
(c) Matched pairs.

Answers
1C 2B 3A 4C
5A 6B 7A 8B

Practice questions:

1. Explain **one** strength and **one** limitation of an independent groups design. *[AS and AL = 2 + 2]*

2. What is meant by the term 'matched pairs design'? Explain **one** limitation of a matched pairs design. *[AS and AL = 2 + 2]*

3. A psychology student decided to carry out a practical using a repeated measures design. But she was concerned about order effects.

   Explain why the student was right to be concerned, and how she could have dealt with the problem. *[AS and AL = 2 + 2]*

Book-link

Y1/AS Student Book
Pages 172–173

Y1/AS Revision Guide
Pages 110–111

A01 **A03**

Topic 7: RESEARCH METHODS

Laboratory experiment

Controlled environment, IV manipulated, effect on DV measured.

⊕ EVs/CVs controlled – demonstrates causation.

⊕ Easily replicated – standardised procedure.

⊖ Low generalisability – artificial, Ps aware of being studied.

⊖ Demand characteristics – cues explain DV.

Field experiment

Natural setting, IV manipulated, effect on DV measured.

⊕ More natural – own environment, generalisable.

⊕ Ps unaware of being studied – more usual behaviour.

⊖ CV control harder – DV changes due to CVs, no cause/effect.

⊖ Ethical issues – no informed consent, invasion of privacy.

Natural experiment

IV varies without researcher, DV naturally occurs or researcher-measured.

⊕ Ethical option – in cases where can't manipulate IV.

⊕ External validity – real-life issues, more relevant.

⊖ Rare natural event – 'one-off', reduces ability to generalise.

⊖ No random allocation – pre-existing IV, CVs.

Quasi-experiment

IV pre-existing difference between people, DV as for natural experiment.

⊕ High control – often lab conditions, cause/effect.

⊕ Comparisons between pre-existing types of people.

⊖ No random allocation – pre-existing IV, CVs.

⊖ No causation – no control over IV, what causes change in DV?

Spec Spotlight

Types of experiment, laboratory and field experiments; natural and quasi-experiments.

1 Which gives the researcher most control over variables?
(a) Laboratory experiment.
(b) Field experiment.
(c) Natural experiment.

2 Which is most affected by demand characteristics?
(a) Laboratory experiment.
(b) Quasi-experiment.
(c) Field experiment.

3 Which does *not* allow cause-and-effect conclusions?
(a) Laboratory experiment.
(b) Field experiment.
(c) Quasi-experiment.

4 Which often takes place in a laboratory?
(a) Quasi-experiment.
(b) Natural experiment.
(c) Field experiment.

5 There is no random allocation to the IV in a:
(a) Laboratory experiment.
(b) Field experiment.
(c) Natural experiment.

6 It can be difficult to get informed consent in a:
(a) Laboratory experiment.
(b) Field experiment.
(c) Quasi-experiment.

7 The DV occurs naturally in a:
(a) Field experiment.
(b) Natural experiment.
(c) Laboratory experiment.

8 The IV occurs without researcher intervention in a:
(a) Laboratory experiment.
(b) Natural experiment.
(c) Field experiment.

Answers
1A 2A 3C 4A
5C 6B 7B 8B

Practice questions:
1. What is meant by the term 'field experiment'? *[AS and AL = 2]*
2. Explain **one** strength and **one** limitation of a laboratory experiment. *[AS and AL = 2 + 2]*
3. Explain **two** strengths of a quasi-experiment. *[AS and AL = 2 + 2]*
4. Explain **one** difference between a field experiment and a natural experiment. *[AS and AL = 2]*

Population	Target group of interest to researcher.
Sample	Smaller subset of population.
Generalisation	Represent population.
Bias	Samples under- or over-represent certain groups.

Random

| Everyone in population equal chance, select via lottery method (e.g. hat). | ⊕ | Potentially unbiased. | ⊖ | Representation not guaranteed. |

Systematic

| Use sampling frame, e.g. every *n*th name from list of target population. | ⊕ | Unbiased, objective. | ⊖ | More time/effort. |

Stratified

| Identify subgroups (strata), select in proportion to numbers in population. | ⊕ | Representative, generalisable. | ⊖ | Imperfect stratification. |

Opportunity

| People easiest/closest to obtain, select by asking people nearby. | ⊕ | Quick, most common. | ⊖ | Inevitably biased. |

Volunteer

| Participants select themselves, select by advert (e.g. on noticeboard). | ⊕ | Willing Ps, more engaged. | ⊖ | Likely biased, e.g. more motivated. |

Spec Spotlight

Sampling: the difference between population and sample; sampling techniques including random, systematic, stratified, opportunity and volunteer; implications of sampling techniques, including bias and generalisation.

1 A sample is _____ the population.
(a) A subset of.
(b) Usually bigger than.
(c) The same size as.

2 Drawing conclusions about a population from the sample is:
(a) Bias.
(b) Generalisation.
(c) Representativeness.

3 The most convenient sampling method is:
(a) Stratified.
(b) Volunteer.
(c) Opportunity.

4 Type of sample where participants select themselves:
(a) Systematic.
(b) Opportunity.
(c) Volunteer.

5 In a random sample:
(a) Everyone has an equal chance of selection.
(b) Subgroups are identified.
(c) A sampling frame is used.

6 An example of a lottery method of selection is:
(a) Drawing names from a container.
(b) Choosing every 20th name from a list.
(c) Putting up an advert.

7 The most representative sampling method is:
(a) Random.
(b) Systematic.
(c) Stratified.

8 A volunteer sample is more _____ than a random sample.
(a) Representative.
(b) Biased.
(c) Generalisable.

Answers
1A 2B 3C 4C
5A 6A 7C 8B

Practice questions:

A psychologist planned to recruit 20 students for a study into conformity, but was unsure which sampling technique to use.

1. Explain **one** difference between a population and a sample. *[AS and AL = 2]*
2. Identify and explain **two** ways in which the psychologist could have selected his participants. *[AS and AL = 3 + 3]*
3. Explain **one** strength and **one** limitation for each technique you have identified. *[AS and AL = 4 + 4]*.

Book-link

Y1/AS Student Book
Pages 176–177

Y1/AS Revision Guide
Page 114

Spec Spotlight

Ethics, including the role of the British Psychological Society's code of ethics; ethical issues in the design and conduct of psychological studies; dealing with ethical issues in research.

A01 Ethical issues		Ways of dealing with them
Ethical issues	Conflict between rights of participants and aims of research.	**BPS Code of Conduct** • Based on respect, competence, responsibility, integrity. • Ethics committees – weigh up costs/benefits.
Informed consent	Participants should make informed decision to take part.	• Presumptive – ask a similar group. • Prior general – agree to be deceived. • Retrospective – get consent after study.
Deception	Misleading/withholding information, means no informed consent.	• Participants debriefed at end of study – told real aims, given full details, told how data to be used, right to withhold data.
Protection from harm	No more risk to participants than in everyday life.	• Right to withdraw at each stage. • Reassured in debriefing about behaviour. • Researcher arranges counselling if needed.
Privacy and confidentiality	Right to control information about self.	• Personal details protected (legal), rarely held. • Refer to participants by number or initials. • Anonymity

1 The ethics of research are regulated by:
(a) Code of Conduct and ethics committees.
(b) Researchers.
(c) The government.

2 For it to mean anything, consent should be:
(a) Temporary.
(b) Informed.
(c) Extracted by force, if necessary.

3 Getting participants' consent to be deceived in advance is:
(a) Presumptive consent.
(b) Retrospective consent.
(c) Prior general consent.

4 Deception can be dealt with by:
(a) Abandoning laboratory experiments.
(b) Not bothering to get consent.
(c) Debriefing participants.

5 Participants can best be protected from harm by:
(a) Giving them the right to withdraw.
(b) Giving them self-defence lessons.
(c) Deceiving them.

6 The risk of harm to participants must be:
(a) Non-existent.
(b) No greater than in ordinary life.
(c) Reasonable.

7 Sometimes a researcher may need to:
(a) Provide counselling.
(b) Cause participants excessive harm.
(c) Refuse to get consent.

8 One way to ensure confidentiality is to:
(a) Share data with other researchers.
(b) Refer to participants by number.
(c) Use participants' full names.

Answers
1A 2B 3C 4C
5A 6B 7A 8B

Topic 7: RESEARCH METHODS

Practice questions:

1. Using an example from psychological research, explain what is meant by 'ethical issue'. *[AS and AL = 3]*

2. Identify and explain **one** ethical issue in psychological research. Briefly outline how this issue could be dealt with. *[AS and AL = 1 + 2 + 3]*

Book-link

Y1/AS Student Book
Pages 180-181
Y1/AS Revision Guide
Pages 116-117

Spec Spotlight

Observational techniques. Types of observation: naturalistic and controlled observation; covert and overt; participant and non-participant observation.

Naturalistic

Takes place where target behaviour would normally occur.

⊕ High external validity, natural.

⊖ Low control – EVs etc.

Controlled

Some control of variables including EVs.

⊕ Replication – standardisation.

⊖ Low external validity.

Covert

Ps unaware of being studied.

⊕ Fewer demand characteristics.

⊖ Ethically questionable.

Overt

Ps aware of being studied.

⊕ More ethically acceptable.

⊖ Some demand characteristics.

Participant

Researcher becomes part of group they are studying.

⊕ Greater insight – experience.

⊖ Possible loss of objectivity.

Non-participant

Researcher remains separate from group they are studying.

⊕ More objective – less bias.

⊖ Loss of insight – too distant.

1 A covert observation can also be:
(a) Non-participant.
(b) Overt.
(c) Controlled.

2 Participants are usually aware they are being studied in:
(a) Novert observation.
(b) Overt observation.
(c) Covert observation.

3 Naturalistic observation:
(a) Takes place where target behaviour normally occurs.
(b) Has control of variables.
(c) Involves the observer becoming part of the group being studied.

4 The observer is most likely to lose their objectivity in:
(a) Naturalistic observation.
(b) Participant observation.
(c) Non-participant observation.

5 The easiest to replicate is:
(a) Simple observation.
(b) Unstructured observation.
(c) Controlled observation.

6 Overt observation is more ethically acceptable than:
(a) Non-participant observation.
(b) Covert observation.
(c) Participant observation.

7 The technique with the fewest extraneous variables is:
(a) Naturalistic observation.
(b) Controlled observation.
(c) Participant observation.

8 Participant observation:
(a) Gives the observer more insight.
(b) Is unbiased.
(c) Suffers from demand characteristics.

Answers
1C 2B 3A 4B
5C 6B 7B 8A

Practice questions:

1. What is meant by the term 'naturalistic observation'? *[AS and AL = 2]*

2. Explain **one** difference between naturalistic observation and controlled observation. *[AS and AL = 2]*

3. Explain **one** strength and **one** limitation of covert observation. *[AS and AL = 2 + 2]*

4. Explain **one** difference between overt observation and participant observation. *[AS and AL = 2]*

Book-link

Y1/AS Student Book
Pages 182-183
(188–189)

Y1/AS Revision Guide
Page 117 (115)

Spec Spotlight

Observational design: behavioural categories; event sampling, time sampling.

Correlations. Analysis of the relationship between covariables. The difference between correlations and experiments. Positive, negative and zero correlations.

Behavioural categories		
Target behaviour broken up into observable categories – operationalisation.	⊖ Difficult to be unambiguous.	⊖ Dustbin categories.
Time sampling		
Observations at regular intervals (e.g. every 15 seconds).	⊕ Reduces observations.	⊖ Miss things outside time frame.
Event sampling		
Target behaviour/event recorded every time it occurs.	⊕ Record infrequent behaviour.	⊖ Complex behaviour oversimplified.

A01	Correlation		A03
Strength and direction between co-variables.			⊕ Useful starting point
Scattergram	One co-variable each axis.		⊕ Relatively economical
Correlation vs experiment	Correlation – no IV manipulated, no cause and effect. Intervening variables uncontrolled (EVs) whereas can be controlled in a lab experiment.		⊖ No cause and effect.
			⊖ Measurement of variables may be unreliable.
Types of correlation	**Positive** – rise/fall together, diagonal line from bottom left to top right. **Negative** – one rise/one fall, diagonal line from bottom right to top left. **Zero** – no correlation.		

Observational design/ Correlation — multiple choice q

1 Observations should be made using:
(a) Cognitive categories.
(b) Emotional categories.
(c) Behavioural categories.

2 In time sampling:
(a) Observations are made at regular intervals.
(b) More observations are made than in event sampling.
(c) All target behaviours are recorded.

3 Event sampling:
(a) Only captures some behaviours.
(b) Oversimplifies behaviours.
(c) Is no use with children.

4 It is important that behavioural categories:
(a) Are ambiguous.
(b) Are clear.
(c) Overlap.

5 In a correlation:
(a) All variables are controlled.
(b) There is a cause-and-effect link.
(c) No IV is manipulated.

6 Both variables increase and decrease together in a:
(a) Positive correlation.
(b) Negative correlation.
(c) Zero correlation.

7 In a negative correlation, the dots on the graph:
(a) Go from top left to bottom right.
(b) Go from bottom left to top right.
(c) Are randomly distributed.

8 In a correlation:
(a) The IV causes the DV.
(b) The DV can cause the IV.
(c) There is no IV or DV.

Answers
1C 2A 3B 4B
5C 6A 7A 8C

Topic 7: RESEARCH METHODS

Practice questions:

A psychologist was studying aggressive behaviour in young children and conducted a controlled observation of them in a school playground.

1. Outline **one** strength and **one** limitation of this study as a controlled observation. *[AS and AL = 2 + 2]*
2. Identify **two** behavioural categories the psychologist could use to measure aggression. *[AS and AL = 1 + 1]*
3. Explain how the psychologist could have used event sampling in this study. *[AS and AL = 2]*

Book-link

Y1/AS Student Book
Pages 184-187

Y1/AS Revision Guide
Page 118-119

Spec Spotlight

Self-report
techniques.
Questionnaires,
interviews, structured
and unstructured.
Questionnaire
construction, including
use of open and closed
questions; design of
interviews.

Topic 7: RESEARCH METHODS

Questionnaires	Pre-set list of written items, can be used to measure DV in experiment.	⊕ Given to lots of people.	⊖ Social desirability bias possible.	
		⊕ Ps more willing to share.	⊖ Response bias possible.	
Interviews	**Structured**			
	Some control of variables including EVs.	⊕ Easy to replicate.	⊖ Interviewers cannot elaborate.	
	Unstructured			
	No set questions, free-flowing face-to-face interaction.	⊕ Points followed up, insight.	⊖ More chance of interviewer bias.	
Design	Avoid jargon, leading questions.	**Closed questions**		
		Limited response choices, quantitative data.	⊕ Easier to analyse.	⊖ Respondents are restricted.
		Open questions		
		Answers given in own words, qualitative data.	⊕ Respondents not restricted.	⊖ Difficult to analyse.

Interviews improved with interview schedule (reduces bias), rapport (relax interviewee), quiet room (interviewee opens up).

1 In completing questionnaires, respondents are:
(a) Prone to social desirability bias.
(b) Always truthful.
(c) Unwilling to share information.

2 In a structured interview, questions are:
(a) Elaborated on.
(b) Presented in a fixed order.
(c) Followed up.

3 The hardest to replicate is:
(a) An unstructured interview.
(b) A structured interview.
(c) A questionnaire.

4 Researcher bias is most likely in:
(a) A questionnaire study.
(b) An unstructured interview.
(c) A structured interview.

5 The most flexible form of self-report is:
(a) A questionnaire.
(b) A structured interview.
(c) An unstructured interview.

6 In questionnaires, the best questions:
(a) Lead the respondent.
(b) Include a double negative.
(c) Avoid jargon words.

7 Closed questions provide data that is:
(a) Quantitative.
(b) Hard to analyse.
(c) Unrestricted.

8 An interviewer can increase rapport by:
(a) Asking the tough questions first.
(b) Helping the interviewee to relax.
(c) Using a questionnaire instead.

Answers 1A 2B 3A 4B 5C 6C 7A 8B

Practice questions:

A researcher wanted to investigate students' experiences of depression. She planned to use a self-report method to collect her data.

1. Write **one** open question and **one** closed question the researcher could use. *[AS and AL = 2 + 2]*
2. Outline **one** strength and **one** limitation of using a structured interview in this study. *[AS and AL = 2 + 2]*
3. The researcher decided to use questionnaire. Outline **two** issues she should take into account when designing the questionnaire. *[AS and AL = 2 + 2]*

Book-link

Y1/AS Student Book
Pages 190-191 (178)
Y1/AS Revision Guide
Page 120 (119)

Spec Spotlight

Quantitative and qualitative data; the distinction between qualitative and quantitative data collection techniques. Primary and secondary data, including meta-analysis.

Pilot studies and the aims of piloting.

Quantitative data				
Numerical data (e.g. reaction time, number of mistakes).	+	Easier to analyse, graphs, etc.	−	Oversimplifies behaviour.
Qualitative data				
Non-numerical data expressed in words (e.g. extracts from diary).	+	Represents complexities.	−	Less easy to analyse, words.
Primary data				
First-hand data collected for purpose of investigation.	+	Tailored to the study itself.	−	Requires times and effort.
Secondary data				
Collected by someone other than person doing the research.	+	Inexpensive, data may exist.	−	Quality may be poor.
Meta-analysis				
Combines data from large number of studies, calculates an effect size.	+	Conclusions greater validity.	−	Publication bias, not all studies.

Pilot studies

Trial run – small-scale test of study procedures before doing real thing.

Aims of piloting – find what does not work before time and money spent

1 **Quantitative data is:**
   (a) Hard to analyse.
   (b) Numerical.
   (c) In the form of words.

2 **A paragraph from a diary is an example of:**
   (a) A meta-analysis.
   (b) Quantitative data.
   (c) Qualitative data.

3 **Which most reflects the complexity of human behaviour?**
   (a) Quantitative data.
   (b) Qualitative data.
   (c) Secondary data.

4 **A researcher has most control over:**
   (a) Primary data.
   (b) Secondary data.
   (c) A meta-analysis.

5 **Secondary data:**
   (a) Is always high quality.
   (b) Already exists.
   (c) Is tailored to the research study.

6 **A meta-analysis:**
   (a) Reduces validity.
   (b) Uses just one study.
   (c) Calculates an effect size.

7 **Failing to include non-significant studies in a meta-analysis:**
   (a) Leads to publication bias.
   (b) Never happens in psychology.
   (c) Makes no difference.

8 **A pilot study is:**
   (a) A small trial of the main study.
   (b) Conducted after the main study.
   (c) Is a kind of research on transportation.

Answers
1B 2C 3B 4A
5B 6C 7A 8A

Practice questions:

1. Outline the difference between quantitative data and qualitative data. *[AS and AL = 3]*
2. Explain **one** strength and **one** limitation of primary data. *[AS and AL = 2 + 2]*
3. Using examples, explain **one** difference between primary data and secondary data. *[AS and AL = 3]*
4. Explain what is meant by 'meta-analysis'. *[AS and AL = 2]*
5. Explain **one** aim of piloting. *[AS and AL = 2]*

Book link

Y1/AS Student Book
Pages 192-195

Y1/AS Revision Guide
Page 121-122

Spec Spotlight

Descriptive statistics: measures of central tendency – mean, median and mode; measures of dispersion – range and standard deviation. Presentation and display of quantitative data: graphs, tables, scattergrams, bar charts, histograms. Distributions: normal and skewed distributions; characteristics of skewed distributions.

Central tendency

Mean

Arithmetic average – add up all scores and divide by number of scores. ⊕ Sensitive – includes all scores. ⊖ May be unrepresentative.

Median

All scores in ascending order, middle value (mean of middle two if even). ⊕ Unaffected by extremes. ⊖ Less sensitive than mean.

Mode

Most frequent/common value, used with categorical/nominal data. ⊕ Relevant to categorical data. ⊖ Overly simple measure.

Dispersion

Range

Difference between highest and lowest values (can add 1). ⊕ Easy to calculate. ⊖ No account of distribution.

Standard deviation

Dispersion of values around mean, larger means more spread out. ⊕ More precise than range. ⊖ Can be misleading.

Display of quantitative data

Tables – raw scores in columns and rows.

Scattergram – continuous data, correlation, data pairs.

Bar chart – categories, bar height represents frequency.

Histogram – data is continuous rather than discrete, true zero.

Distributions

Normal distribution – mean, median, mode all together.

Negative skew – most scores higher (e.g. easy test).

Positive skew – most scores lower (e.g. hard test).

1 Mean, median and mode are measures of:
(a) Dispersion.
(b) Central tendency.
(c) Spread.

2 The middle value of a set of data is the:
(a) Mean.
(b) Median.
(c) Mode.

3 The most sensitive measure of central tendency is:
(a) Mean.
(b) Median.
(c) Mode.

4 The average to use with categorical data is the:
(a) Mean.
(b) Mode.
(c) Median.

5 The median _____ than the mean.
(a) Is harder to calculate.
(b) Includes more data.
(c) Is less affected by extreme values.

6 The range:
(a) Does not take distribution of values into account.
(b) Is very hard to calculate.
(c) Is more precise than the standard deviation.

7 Mean, median and mode are the same in a:
(a) Negatively skewed distribution.
(b) Positively skewed distribution.
(c) Normal distribution.

8 The graph used to represent correlation is a:
(a) Scattergram.
(b) Bar chart.
(c) Histogram.

Answers
1B 2B 3A 4B
5C 6A 7C 8A

Practice questions:

1. Explain what is meant by 'measure of dispersion'. *[AS and AL = 2]*
2. Explain how a researcher would calculate a median. *[AS and AL = 2]*
3. Outline **one** strength and **one** limitation of using the mode as a measure of central tendency. *[AS and AL = 2 + 2]*
4. What is meant by the term 'standard deviation'? *[AS and AL = 2]*
5. Explain **one** limitation of using the range as a measure of dispersion. *[AS and AL = 2]*

Percentages	Percentage means 'divide by 100'.
Percentage to decimal	Remove % sign, move decimal point two places to left.
Decimal to fraction	If 2 decimal places denominator is 100, 3 places then 1000, etc. Reduce fraction by finding highest common factor.
Ratios	Part-to-part, e.g. ratio of one part of a class to another. Part-to-whole, e.g. ratio of one part of class to whole class.
Decimal places	Number of digits to right of decimal point.
Significant figures	$0.002473691 = 0.002$ (1 s.f.) or 0.0025 (2 s.f.) – rounding off.
Standard form	Large/small numbers – $3.2 \times 10^5 = 320{,}000$; $3.2 \times 10^{-5} = 0.000032$

Spec Spotlight

Mathematical
requirements, see full
list in AS/Y1 Revision
Guide, page 123.

$=$	equals	$>$	greater than	$<$	less than
$\approx$	approximately equal to	$>>$	much greater than	$<<$	much less than
α	proportional to				

Mathematical requirements – multiple choice questions

1 What does percentage mean?
(a) Divide by 100.
(b) Multiply by 100.
(c) Subtract 100.

2 Converting a percentage to a decimal involves moving the decimal point:
(a) Two places to the right.
(b) One place to the right.
(c) Two places to the left.

3 When converting to a fraction, you should always:
(a) Have a nice cup of tea afterwards.
(b) Find the highest common factor.
(c) Find the highest common numerator.

4 There are two types of ratio, which are:
(a) Part-to-whole, part-to-part.
(b) Heart-to-whole, heart-to-heart.
(c) Chart-to-whole, chart-to-chart.

5 Converting to significant figures involves:
(a) Rounding up and down.
(b) Always rounding down.
(c) Always rounding up.

6 A way of expressing very large and small numbers is:
(a) Percentages.
(b) Fractions.
(c) Standard form.

7 >> means:
(a) Less than.
(b) Proportional to.
(c) Much greater than.

8 ≈ means:
(a) Equals.
(b) Approximately equal to.
(c) Danger! Rough seas!.

Topic 7: RESEARCH METHODS

Answers
1A 2C 3B 4A
5A 6C 7C 8B

Practice questions:

1. Donald completed a questionnaire to measure authoritarian personality. There were 40 items, and 16 of Donald's responses indicated he had an authoritarian personality.
   Express this outcome as (a) a percentage, (b) a decimal, (c) a fraction, and (d) a ratio. *[AS and AL = 4]*

2. Kim scored 38. Use the appropriate mathematical symbol(s) to express the relationship between Donald's and Kim's scores. *[1 mark]*

Significance	Difference/ association due to chance?	Conditions of use	Difference in scores, related items, nominal data (or better).
Probability	Accepted level $p = 0.05$.	Calculation	1. Sign of difference between condition A and B.
Calculated value	Outcome of test.		2. Calculate total + and –
Critical value	Look up in table.		3. Total of less frequent sign (S).
Finding critical value	Need: significance level, N or df, one- or two-tailed.		4. Ignore participants with same score A and B.
		Critical value	Calculated S equal to or less than critical value, decide to accept/ reject null hypothesis.

Topic 7: RESEARCH METHODS

Spec Spotlight

Introduction to statistical testing: the sign test.

The role of peer review in the scientific process. The implications of psychological research for the economy.

AO3   **Peer review/Psychology and economy**   **AO1**

Peer review

⊕ Protect quality of research.

⊕ May criticise rival research.

⊖ Publication bias.

⊖ Ground breaking research buried.

Psychology and the economy

Findings of research benefit economic prosperity.

- Attachment – role of father, flexible working, parents contribute to economy.
- Treatment of mental illness – work days lost from depression, effective treatments contribute to economy.

1 The commonly accepted level of significance in psychology is:
(a) $p = 0.5$
(b) $p = 0.005$
(c) $p = 0.05$

2 When determining significance of a data set, a calculated value is compared with a:
(a) Key value.
(b) Critical value.
(c) Significant value.

3 The sign test is used for _____ between two sets of scores.
(a) A difference.
(b) A correlation.
(c) An association.

4 The test used for a directional hypothesis is a:
(a) One-tailed test.
(b) Two-tailed test.
(c) Three-tailed test.

5 Peer review:
(a) Is always objective.
(b) Sometimes ignores ground-breaking research.
(c) Guarantees high-quality research.

6 Psychology can benefit economic prosperity:
(a) Through the findings of research.
(b) Only in very narrow areas.
(c) But only in the short term.

7 Attachment research:
(a) Has no benefits for the economy.
(b) Undermines the role of the father.
(c) Promotes flexible working.

8 Research into depression helps the economy because:
(a) Diagnosis is slower.
(b) Treatment may be better.
(c) People spend more time off work.

Answers
1C 2B 3A 4A
5B 6A 7C 8B

Practice questions:

1. Identify the **three** pieces of information you need to find a critical value. *[AS and AL = 3]*
2. What is meant by the term 'peer review'? *[AS and AL = 2]*
3. Briefly discuss the role of peer review in the scientific process. *[AS and AL = 6]*
4. Using an example, outline the implications of psychological research for the economy. *[AS and AL = 4]*

Y2/A Student Book
Pages 63–65

Y2/A Revision Guide
Page 45–46

Correlation coefficient

Number between –1 and +1.

Strength = the closer to 1 (plus or minus) the stronger the correlation.

Direction = sign, '+' is positive correlation, '–' is negative.

+1 is perfect positive correlation, –1 is perfect negative correlation.
$r = +.5$ is just as strong as $r = -.5$, r is symbol for coefficient.

Scattergrams

See page 127.

Spec Spotlight

Analysis and interpretation of correlation, including correlation coefficients.

Case studies.

Topic 7: RESEARCH METHODS

A01	Case studies	A03
Detailed in-depth study of individual/group/institution/event, longitudinal.		⊕ Rich detailed insight.
Unusual cases (e.g. rare disorder), typical cases (e.g. childhood memories).		⊕ Allows study of both unusual and typical behaviour.
Qualitative (e.g. interviews) and quantitative data (e.g. psychological tests).		⊖ Prone to researcher bias.
		⊖ Participants' accounts biased.

A level only

Correlation/Case studies – *multiple choice questions*

1 The numerical measure of correlation is called the:
  (a) Correlation efficient.
  (b) Correlation coefficient.
  (c) Correlation deficient.

2 Correlation is measured in terms of its:
  (a) Length and breadth.
  (b) Strength and direction.
  (c) Height and depth.

3 $r = -1.0$ can be described as a:
  (a) Weak negative correlation.
  (b) Zero correlation.
  (c) Perfect negative correlation.

4 $r = +0.5$ is _____ $r = -0.5$.
  (a) Just as strong as.
  (b) A stronger correlation than.
  (c) Much stronger than.

5 A case study can be a study of:
  (a) Only individuals.
  (b) Individuals and groups.
  (c) Individuals, groups and organisations.

6 Case studies investigate:
  (a) Unusual cases only.
  (b) Typical cases only.
  (c) Both unusual and typical cases.

7 Case studies produce:
  (a) Qualitative and quantitative data.
  (b) Only quantitative data.
  (c) Only qualitative data.

8 Case studies tend to take place:
  (a) Mostly in laboratories.
  (b) Over a longer period than most research methods.
  (c) For just a brief time.

Answers
1B 2B 3C 4A
5C 6C 7A 8B

Topic 7: RESEARCH METHODS

Practice questions:

A psychologist measured the relationship between hours spent at work and level of stress. She found a correlation coefficient of +.65.

1. Describe what this tells us about the nature of the relationship between work and stress. *[AS and AL = 4]*
2. Explain what is meant by the term 'correlation coefficient'. *[AS and AL = 2]*
3. Referring to **one** example that you have studied, briefly outline and evaluate the use of case studies in psychology. *[AS and AL = 8]*

Book-link

Y2/A Student Book
Pages 64-65

Y2/A Revision Guide
Page 47

Spec Spotlight

Content analysis
and coding.
Thematic analysis

Content analysis

Indirect study of communications.

Form of observation – of spoken interaction and/or written communications, examples from media.

Coding

Quantitative data.

Categorise information into meaningful units – e.g. number of words or phrases.

Thematic analysis

Qualitative data.

Recurrent ideas – keep 'cropping up', more descriptive than coding units, broader categories (e.g. 'stereotyping').

$\oplus$ Ethical issues avoided – e.g. consent not always needed.

$\oplus$ Flexible method – adapt to aims of research (quantitative or qualitative).

$\ominus$ Communication studied out of context – reduces validity.

$\ominus$ May lack objectivity – choice of categories may depend on researcher's personal views.

Topic 7: RESEARCH METHODS

A level only

(142)

Content analysis, coding and thematic analysis – *multiple choice questions*

1 Content analysis is a form of:
(a) Questionnaire.
(b) Laboratory experiment.
(c) Observational study.

2 Content analysis investigates behaviour:
(a) Directly.
(b) Indirectly.
(c) In a social context.

3 Coding tends to produce data that is:
(a) Quantitative.
(b) Qualitative.
(c) Hard to analyse.

4 Thematic analysis is _____ than coding units.
(a) Less descriptive.
(b) More specific.
(c) More descriptive.

5 In content and thematic analysis:
(a) Many ethical issues are avoided.
(b) There are no ethical issues.
(c) Consent is usually an issue.

6 Content and thematic analysis are:
(a) Hard to adapt to research aims.
(b) Flexible methods.
(c) Highly inflexible.

7 Studying communication out of its original context:
(a) Reduces validity.
(b) Increases validity.
(c) Has no effect on validity.

8 Compared to content analysis, thematic analysis is probably:
(a) Less biased.
(b) Less objective.
(c) More objective.

Topic 7: RESEARCH METHODS

Answers
1C 2B 3A 4C
5A 6B 7A 8B

Practice questions:

1. Explain **one** difference between content analysis and thematic analysis. *[AS and AL = 2]*
2. Briefly outline content analysis **and/or** thematic analysis. *[AS and AL = 4]*
3. Briefly evaluate content analysis as a research method in psychology. *[AS and AL = 5]*
4. Explain **one** strength and **one** limitation of content analysis. *[AS and AL = 2 + 2]*

Book-link

Y2/A Student Book
Pages 66-69

Y2/A Revision Guide
Page 48-49

Spec Spotlight

Reliability across all methods of investigation. Ways of assessing reliability: test-retest and interobserver; improving reliability. Types of validity across all methods of investigation: face validity, concurrent validity, ecological validity and temporal validity. Assessment of validity. Improving validity.

Reliability

Measure of *consistency*.

Test-retest – test same people twice.

Interobserver – compare observations from different observers.

Correlation coefficient – two sets of scores should correlate at least +.8 for reliability.

Improving reliability

Questionnaires – rewrite questions.

Interviews – improve training.

Experiments – standardise procedure.

Observations – operationalise behavioural categories.

Validity

Measure of *legitimacy* (genuine effect).

Ecological validity – findings generalise to other settings (e.g. everyday life).

Temporal validity – findings remain true over time (not historically specific, e.g. Asch).

Face validity – test looks like it measures what it should (basic, 'eyeballing').

Concurrent validity – findings similar to well-established test (coefficient > +.8).

Improving validity

Experiments – use control group and standardised procedure.

Questionnaires – use lie scale and ensure confidentiality.

Observations – well-defined behavioural categories, no overlap.

Qualitative – use interpretive validity and triangulation (different sources).

Topic 7: RESEARCH METHODS

A level only

Reliability and validity – *multiple choice questions*

1 Reliability measures:
(a) Accuracy.
(b) Consistency.
(c) Legitimacy.

2 Testing the same people twice is:
(a) Test-detest reliability.
(b) Test-test reliability.
(c) Test-retest reliability.

3 For reliability, the correlation coefficient needs to be:
(a) Up to +.8
(b) At least –.8
(c) Over +.8

4 One way to improve the reliability of experiments is to:
(a) Use standardised procedures.
(b) Improve training of interviewers.
(c) Rewrite questionnaire items.

5 Being able to generalise research findings to other settings is:
(a) Temporal validity.
(b) Concurrent validity.
(c) Ecological validity.

6 In the context of validity, 'eyeballing' is a practice that relates to:
(a) Concurrent validity.
(b) Staring at someone very intensely.
(c) Face validity.

7 The validity of a questionnaire can be improved by using:
(a) A lie scale.
(b) Interpretative validity.
(c) Test-retest.

8 You can improve the validity of qualitative research by using:
(a) A control group.
(b) Triangulation.
(c) Well-defined behavioural categories.

Answers
1B 2C 3C 4A
5C 6C 7A 8B

Topic 7: RESEARCH METHODS

Practice questions:

A team of clinical psychologists developed a questionnaire to measure stress in A level students.

1. Outline **one** way in which the psychologists could establish the reliability of their questionnaire. *[AS and AL = 3]*

2. Describe how the psychologists could improve the reliability of the questionnaire. *[AS and AL = 3]*

3. Choose **one other** research method and explain how the validity of that method could be improved. *[AS and AL = 3]*

Book-link

Y2/A Student Book
Pages 70–80

Y2/A Revision Guide
Page 50–53

Spec Spotlight

Factors affecting the choice of statistical test, including level of measurement and experimental design. When to use the following tests: Spearman's rho, Pearson's r, Wilcoxon, Mann–Whitney, related t-test, unrelated t-test and Chi-squared test. Probability and significance: use of statistical tables and critical values in interpretation of significance; Type I and Type II errors

Choice of statistical test

Three decisions to make:	Test of difference		Test of association or correlation
	Unrelated	Related	
Nominal	Chi-squared	Sign test	Chi-square
Ordinal	Mann–Whitney	Wilcoxon	Spearman's rho
Interval	Unrelated t-test	Related t-test	Pearson's r

Probability and significance

Statistical table – compare calculated and critical value (see page 137).

$p \leq 0.05$ means the probability that the observed effect (the result) occurred by chance equal to/less than 5%.

Type I and II errors

Type I error – null hypothesis rejected when 'true,' optimistic.

Type II error – null hypothesis accepted when 'false', pessimistic.

Type I more likely – significance level too lenient (eg. $p = 0.1$).

Type II more likely – significance level too stringent (eg. $p = 0.01$).

Levels of measurement

Nominal – frequency data in categories (e.g. favourite team).

Ordinal – data in order, intervals subjective (e.g. rate on 1 to 10 scale).

Interval – data measured on units of equal size (e.g. metres or minutes).

NB You should also be familiar with the use of inferential tests, i.e. you may be asked to make a simple calculation with a formula.

A level only

Statistical testing and probability – *multiple choice questions*

1 Number of decisions to make to choose a statistical test:
(a) 3
(b) 4
(c) 5

2 'Nominal, ordinal or interval' refers to:
(a) Level of measurement.
(b) Experimental design.
(c) Level of significance.

3 Difference, ordinal and unrelated – the appropriate test is:
(a) Wilcoxon.
(b) Unrelated *t*-test.
(c) Mann–Whitney.

4 Data measured on a scale of subjective intervals is:
(a) Nominal.
(b) Ordinal.
(c) Interval.

5 When a statistical test is significant, the:
(a) Research hypothesis is rejected.
(b) Null hypothesis is accepted.
(c) Null hypothesis is rejected.

6 $p \leq 0.05$ refers to the probability that the observed effect occurred by chance is:
(a) Equal to 5%
(b) Less than or equal to 5%
(c) More than or equal to 5%

7 The null hypothesis is rejected when it is really true. This is a:
(a) Type III error.
(b) Type II error.
(c) Type I error.

8 A stringent level of significance makes a _____ more likely.
(a) Type I error.
(b) Type II error.
(c) Type I and Type II error.

Answers
1A 2A 3C 4B
5C 6B 7C 8B

Practice questions:
1. Give **three** reasons why a researcher would use a Pearson's *r* statistical test. *[AS and AL = 3]*
2. Explain what is meant by 'level of measurement'. *[AS and AL = 2]*
3. Explain what is meant by the phrase 'the result of the statistical test was significant at $p < 0.05$'. *[AS and AL = 2]*
4. Briefly outline the difference between a Type I and Type II error. *[AS and AL = 3]*

Book-link

Y2/A Student Book
Pages 81–83

Y2/A Revision Guide
Page 54–55

Spec Spotlight

Reporting psychological investigations. Sections of a scientific report: abstract, introduction, method, results, Discussion and referencing. Features of science: objectivity and the empirical method; replicability and falsifiability; theory construction and hypothesis testing; paradigms and paradigm shifts.

(147)

Reporting investigations

Abstract – short summary, main parts.

Introduction – review of literature, logical progression to hypothesis.

Method – design, sample, materials, procedure, ethics, detailed replication.

Results – descriptive and inferential statistics (tests), raw data in appendix.

Discussion – summary, links to earlier research, limitations, implications.

Referencing – use standard format, e.g.
Jones, R. (2001) The test. *Basic Journal*, 4(1), 23–27.
Jones, R. (2001) *The test*. London: Books

Features of science

Objectivity – researchers maintain distance, unbiased.

Replicability – findings repeatable across contexts, generalisable.

Theory construction – general law, derive and test hypothesis.

Empirical method – data collected through direct sensory experience.

Falsifiability – theories must be held up for testing, possibly proved false.

Paradigms/shifts – psychology pre-science, lacks a paradigm (Kuhn).

Topic 7: RESEARCH METHODS

Reporting investigations/Features of science – *multiple choice questions*

1 There are __ main sections to an investigation report.
(a) 4
(b) 5
(c) 6

2 'A short summary of the main parts' is a description of the:
(a) Abstract.
(b) Introduction.
(c) Method.

3 Limitations of a study are reported in the:
(a) Introduction.
(b) References.
(c) Discussion.

4 Raw data should go in the:
(a) Results.
(b) Appendix.
(c) Discussion.

5 According to Thomas Kuhn, psychology:
(a) Is a fully-fledged science.
(b) Lacks a paradigm.
(c) Is at the post-science stage.

6 'Being able to derive hypotheses for testing' is a description of:
(a) Theory construction.
(b) A paradigm shift.
(c) Falsifiability.

7 To be a science, theories in psychology need to be:
(a) False.
(b) Falsifiable.
(c) True.

8 Any method of collecting data directly through the senses is:
(a) Replicable.
(b) Objective.
(c) Empirical.

Topic 7: RESEARCH METHODS

Answers
1C 2A 3C 4B
5B 6A 7B 8C

Practice questions:

1. In relation to reporting investigations, explain what is meant by the 'method'. *[AS and AL = 4]*

2. Outline what should be included in the discussion section of a report of a psychological investigation. *[AS and AL = 4]*

3. Briefly describe **two** features of science. *[AS and AL = 2 + 2]*

4. Distinguish between falsifiability and objectivity in relation to features of science. *[AS and AL = 3]*

NOTES